ADVANCE PRAISE FOR *UNDER (*

I'm beyond sure that *this* book will smooth the road for countless families who face the daunting task of re-combining their lives under one roof. Newman shows you how to traverse that road to get there, and how much better you all will be for the journey.

In this economy, more newlyweds and engaged couples see the enormous financial advantages of moving back under one roof with a set of parents, perhaps (gulp!) the *in-laws* . . . thus opening the proverbial can of concerns about privacy, lifestyle, etc. And then of course, there's the sobering reality faced by many couples just starting their lives together—a parent or parents might need special care, or lose a job, or divorce or be widowed.

As your guide through the jungle of moving in with Mom and Dad—or moving Mom and Dad *in*—Susan Newman provides a master class in establishing boundaries, setting realistic expectations, handling the reversion into childhood roles and strategies, manipulations, and guilt. Real and brilliant.

—Sharon Naylor, author of *Home from the Honeymoon*

In 21st century America, where many adults, sometimes with kids in tow, find themselves moving back in with their parents, here comes a loving, practical, and well-paced book on how several generations can successfully live together—again. Susan Newman not only provides a "how-to" guide for every imaginable glitch that can and will arise, but she—well—she makes it seem fun, adventurous, and a compassionate journey full of surprises, joys, and challenges—where families will work things out lovingly; for family love endures while other loves dissipate or break down. There's no notion of reentry failure here, for as Dr. Newman points out, multigenerational American families were once the norm, and it's the post-World II nuclear family that is the anomaly.

As a Chinese American, multigenerational households are familiar territory. Still, I know it's tricky business, and even I would want this book sitting front and center on our living room coffee table if I were to live this way again. And one on the breakfast table and another on the bookshelf and yet another in . . . in fact, everyone under my roof would have their own well-thumbed copy!

—William Poy Lee, author of *The Eighth Promise*

In *Under One Roof Again,* Dr. Susan Newman provides well-researched, detailed, insightful, and empowering advice to all parties of the "back living at home again" equation. This long overdue, up-to-date innovative book will normalize, infuse dignity, inspire hope, and offer concrete expert advice for the ever-changing needs of the dynamically evolving, all too human institution called "family." I highly recommend this outstanding book to all families facing the demands and challenges of having loved ones of all ages who return home.

 —Jeffrey Bernstein, PhD, psychologist and author of *Liking the Child You Love*

As our challenging economy forces more people than ever to move back in with their relatives, Susan Newman performs an extraordinary service by guiding us through the complexities of intergenerational living, identifying the potential landmines, and offering suggestions for defusing them. From dating, to housekeeping, to regression, *Under One Roof Again* culls real stories from real people and explores the many issues that can plague boomerang families.

 —Jim Axelrod, national correspondent for CBS News

Dr. Susan Newman has written a compelling guide for parents and their adult children who are faced with the new family dynamics of all living together. During these difficult times, her down-to-earth, straightforward book couldn't be more timely because it deals with the sensitive issues that crop up in unanticipated living arrangements. Her insights and advice, especially involving multigenerational households, offer reassurance and guidance to turn these changing relationships into stronger, more loving family units.

 —Allan Zullo, co-author, *A Boomer's Guide to Grandparenting*

They're baaaaaaaaack! Fortunately, life with your grown-up kids returned home doesn't have to be a horror movie—at least, not after you read this book! (And, of course, after you leave it next to the milk and cookies for when the dear ones get home.)

 —Lenore Skenazy, founder, www.freerangekids.com
 and author of *Free-Range Kids*

A valuable resource for when the empty nest becomes full again.

 —Joshua Piven, co-author, *The Worst-Case Scenario Survival Handbooks*

Learning to live with another person entails negotiating a relationship that is mutually beneficial and satisfying. In this timely and inspiring book, social psychologist Dr. Susan Newman offers life lessons for family members who, for a variety of reasons, face the trepidation of living under the same roof again with younger or older relatives. Filled with relatable anecdotes and sage advice, this practical book will help readers define and set boundaries, and make the necessary compromises they need to live together harmoniously.

Under One Roof Again is particularly relevant to the times but the information and advice it offers is timeless. With her unique understanding of relationships and of the social context, Dr. Newman's message is reassuring and reverses the conventional wisdom that coming home is a burden. It shows how the new normal can, instead, enrich the lives of parents and their adult children.

—Irene S. Levine, PhD, professor of psychiatry, New York University
School of Medicine, and author of *Best Friends Forever*

What do you say when your parent starts grilling you on your social life? What are some of the ways an employed offspring can contribute to family living expenses? "Interacting with parents, relatives and grown-up children is a balancing act which requires special insights," writes Susan Newman in this wonderfully insightful and comprehensive book in which she covers both the macro and micro issues that arise in multigenerational living arrangements.

From the big challenges like how not to get stuck in the parent-child trap because it works both ways—parents continue to parent, children act like their 10-year-old selves—to minor hurdles like introducing a new person into the family, Dr. Newman has important, timely advice.

—Susan Ginsberg, EdD, Editor/Publisher of the *Work & Family Life* newsletter
(workandfamilylife.com) and author of *Family Wisdom*

Under One Roof Again is such a timely, helpful, and upbeat guide for the many parents and children who find themselves living together again. Newman, by interviewing hundreds of subjects, has put her finger on the essential things they need to know. She offers guidelines for attitude changes, the available options in many situations, such as time and money dilemmas, and covers each person's expectations giving you helpful clues to what your family members may be thinking. A really important aide for families in this situation, guaranteed to help them create a comfortable and mutually happy situation out of dire necessity.

—Tina B. Tessina, PhD, psychotherapist and author of *Money, Sex and Kids*

UNDER ONE ROOF AGAIN

All Grown Up and (Re)learning
to Live Together Happily

SUSAN NEWMAN, PhD

LYONS PRESS

Guilford, Connecticut

An imprint of Globe Pequot Press

Lyons Press is an imprint of Globe Pequot Press

Text design: Sheryl P. Kober
Layout: Joanna Beyer

Library of Congress Cataloging-in-Publication Data is available on file.

ISBN 978-0-7627-5859-3

Printed in the United States of America

10 9 8 7 6 5 4 3 2 1

The material in this book is intended to provide accurate and authoritative information but should not be used as a substitute for professional care. The author and publisher urge you to consult with your mental health care provider or seek other professional advice in the event that you require expert assistance.

For Richard, my ardent cheerleader

Contents

CONTENTS

CONTENTS

Author's Note

How does an atom split? Can global warming be mastered? How does a homing pigeon know where to "home"? What keeps an airplane up in the sky? All perplexing phenomena for most people. If you are not an expert in a particular field, comprehending or managing a remarkable occurrence falls somewhere between difficult and impossible.

How families function, like so many incidents we try to understand, is often inexplicable, too. When a family comes together as adults sharing the same space, it is harder to explain and usually more complicated than when parents are raising young children. In order to sort through the complexities, I questioned over 200 people—close to 100 for *Under One Roof Again,* combined with 150 from research for a previous book on adult children–parent relationships. The results from these two research studies offer a large sample and vivid pictures of situations with which you will identify in the chapters that most closely match your current circumstances. While names have been changed to protect identities, the stories are genuine, and the feelings they reveal are poignant and enlightening.

The "voices" you read represent different age groups, different family relationships, and different cultures; they span the country from Puerto Rico to California. I talked with men and women as young as twenty-two and seniors who celebrated their eightieth birthday a good while ago. Statisticians would categorize some as well-to-do, some middle-income, and others barely getting by monetarily.

People told me about their relationships with their mothers, fathers, sons, daughters, in-laws, and siblings in great detail. They shared the difficulties that they were having or had when moving in together, and how they worked them out—or didn't. In short, they reported the good and the bad: the taxing and stressful aspects of living with a close relative again as adults, along with enthusiastic accounts of what they felt were the immediate benefits and long-range rewards.

It is their collective contributions—their thoughts and problems—that form the heart of this book, and from them I found *answers* to the question, Can close relatives live together successfully as adults? "Answers" is plural because no set rule, single line of reasoning, or course of action produces the same result in every family. Each family is a wonderful and unique phenomenon to be figured out individually, by and for its members, depending on their individual needs.

Every person I contacted made a contribution that will help you resolve difficulties you have or may encounter at some point, before or while living together again. The insights and practical information they volunteered provide the backbone for the advice and suggestions that appear throughout this book.

I want to learn what was useful to you and your family as you share your home for the second, or perhaps third, time. You can reach me by e-mail through the contact link on my Web site (www.susannewmanphd.com); I will respond to your comments or questions.

Wishing you well on your family (re)connection experience,
Susan Newman, PhD

Introduction

"What—you didn't change the locks?" is one of many attempts at humor you may hear when telling a friend your adult child or parent is coming to live with you. Similarly, you might hear, "Are you crazy?" when you announce that you are leaving town to live with your son or daughter. "Good luck!" is often tacked on rather snidely, as if there weren't a chance in the world these new arrangements could work.

My variation on the same theme is a parent saying to her adult child: "What? You left work early. Isn't that risky? You'll lose your job and have to live with us again." Every time my twenty-seven-year-old son tells me anything he's done that I think might jeopardize his job in the slightest, I react this way. It's only natural; I'm his mother.

He doesn't want to return home, and I'm not sure I would want him back living with me full-time. That was until I understood the upside of living under the same roof again; how attitudes about family have changed; and how the economy is altering the face of family. Almost no field is a sure thing for finding or keeping a job these days. Even the traditional, "forever" jobs in teaching and health care have faced upheaval and massive employment reductions.

Whether you are twenty-six or sixty-six years old, it increasingly takes more money to maintain your lifestyle. Alterations in the job market—including shifts in entire industries, ups and downs in the stock market, difficulty getting loans, credit card debt, and high housing and health-care costs—have put a new spin on almost everyone's options. Things happen. Things change. That's how life is.

If you're holding on to the antiquated negative attitude toward moving in with family, you'll miss a great opportunity to be part of the current cultural shift. Family represents your most enduring lifetime relationships. Living under one roof again gives you the chance to enhance those relationships and make them stronger and more positive. For millions, these new circumstances work. More and more people are learning to live harmoniously with their family members, and, as you will see, it is not that difficult.

Live Together? "Unthinkable!"

A hundred years ago, families stuck together; in fact, most family members rarely left home. During the Great Depression and for years afterward, families stayed in close proximity—moving within a five-mile radius of where they grew up—or lived together in different configurations. My paternal grandparents lived in the same house with my great-aunt and -uncle, sharing one bathroom and the kitchen. My own parents stayed with my maternal grandparents until I was born, five years after my brother. Four people were too many for the tiny room in my grandparents' home, and we moved into our own house six blocks away and around the corner from my father's parents.

In the ensuing decades families started to disperse, and with migration came profound social change. Young and old followed their jobs wherever they took them; Elvis and then the Beatles prevailed; and drug use proliferated, serving to redefine America and give birth to the first real generation gap. During the 1960s, the majority of Americans felt it would be "unthinkable" to have their adult sons and daughters return home, or to have their parents move in with them. Independence was a crucial, strived-for virtue.

In those years, and until quite recently, offspring were viewed as failures and their parents seen as enablers if their children didn't grow up to find jobs and live on their own, or if their divorced sons and daughters returned to the nest. Parents were thought to have done a "good job" if their high school and college graduates functioned and thrived hundreds, even thousands, of miles away from them. Parents moved in with their adult children only in special circumstances—for example, if one parent had died and the surviving parent had a hard time functioning on his or her own, or if the parent needed health care. That was then. Families today are reuniting under one roof in record numbers. Independence is no longer the gold standard, and the stigma of adult children of any age returning home or living with parents in their house—or yours—has vanished.

Families today are reuniting under one roof in record numbers.

"BOOMERANG" GETS A NEW DEFINITION

Coming back home or moving a relative into yours means living with family members with whom you thought you would only share visits, holidays, or the occasional vacation. In one fashion or another, you or someone you love is boomeranging. The term *boomerang* itself has expanded from its previous meaning—a college grad who returned home to live. Now a boomeranging person is just as likely to be a fifty-year-old parent or a seventy-five-year-old grandparent; a midlife adult with a family in tow, or a twenty-eight-year-old trying to figure out what she wants to do next. Siblings boomerang to bunk with another sibling who is willing to bail them out of a personal predicament. Boomerang relatives of all ages number in the millions, and, if you're reading this book, you are probably one of them—or about to be—and this book will help make that "new" living situation relationship a success.

You, your son or daughter, or your sister or brother may have just finished college and can't find a job. Education loans for some run over $100,000, and paying them back may prevent you from living on your own. Credit card debt may also be sapping reserves that you would normally use for housing. Perhaps you have a decent paying job but want to save to buy an apartment or home, or to go back to school for an advanced degree. Over 1.5 million students graduated from college in 2009, and more than three-quarters of them flocked back to family for a hoped-for six-month stint that invariably turns into a few or many years.

Maybe you had a baby that you hadn't planned for, and need your family for financial and emotional support. If you are a single parent, your own parents' presence can make sanity possible. Your company may have downsized, cutting you and the paycheck that paid your rent or mortgage. Perhaps you're a grandparent, and your son or daughter could use your support, so you are moving in to help out, or have done so already. Many of the estimated 56 million grandparents in the U.S. want to assist their sons and daughters, and Marian Robinson's move into the White House to care for her granddaughters has put a national "seal of approval" on that living arrangement.

It may be that you have realized closing off rooms to save on heat bills and rattling around in a house too large for one or two isn't fun anymore. You might decide to invite an offspring to "room" with you, or sell your home and live with them. Or perhaps you've retired and have time on your hands; your spouse of many years has died, and you want the comfort and company of your children, and to help with your grandchildren. Maybe you are divorcing or already divorced, and you can't make payments on two places. Whatever the reason for the change of residence, you are part of the newly defined boomerang generation.

MULTIGENERATIONAL FAMILIES MAKE A COMEBACK

According to the 2003 census, almost one-fourth of those who moved that year cited "family" as the reason for their move; that's more than those who said their move was job-related. In light of recent attitude shifts, this proclaimed reason is not so surprising. Before the real estate collapse in 2008, multigenerational communities were sprouting up across the country because grandparents wanted to be near their children and grandchildren, siblings wanted to continue their relationships, and because closeness offered peace of mind, eliminating the worry about aging parents who lived great distances away.

Not since the Great Depression have we seen so many families turning to their immediate relatives as a lifeline. A return to the way we lived a hundred years ago—when people rarely left home, when family members were vital for working farmland, is under way. Family constellations are being altered—some temporarily, others permanently. U.S. household data reflects a steady

Not since the Great Depression have we seen so many families turning to their immediate relatives as a lifeline.

increase in parents living with their adult children and adult children moving in with parents. As of January 2009, AARP and the U.S. Census Bureau estimate the number of multigenerational households at 6.2 million and growing. For the most part, those who move in together are enjoying their lives—lives made less stressful and more manageable by their new living arrangements.

What I found particularly striking was a mini rant from a thirty-year-old single woman I interviewed. Olivia asked a lot of rhetorical questions to make her point: "What's wrong in our culture that we Caucasians don't get along with our families? Immigrant families from many cultures—Latino, black, Asian—have had the generations living together forever. Why can't the rest of us love and support our relatives in the same way? A lot of people are sharing living expenses with friends; why not move in with your family?" asks Olivia, who is delighted to be living with her parents again.

Coming together as a family isn't new, as Olivia points out. Immigrant families have been living together since they started coming to America. In many different cultures, second- and third-generation relatives who grew up in America don't move far from parents; they remain faithful to family and the patterns of their culture of origin. Seventy-nine percent of first- and second-generation Latinos, for example, believe "it is better for children to live in their parents' home until they get married," according to The Pew Hispanic Center. The same survey of generational differences found that Latin Americans think "relatives are more important than friends"—92 percent of first-generation; 82 percent of second-generation; and 81 percent of third-generation Latinos.

Today, first- and second-generation immigrant families are likely to be two-parent households, but they also are likely to include grandparents, other relatives, and nonrelatives who provide nurturing and economic support to the family. It is not unusual for several generations to live in one house or apartment. Grandparents, parents, siblings, daughters- and sons-in-law—they all stand by each other and celebrate the good and bad times together. They are role models for the rest of us.

Mutual Admiration Society

And while immigrant families have been sticking together for decades, others have spent the years working (and hoping) to raise self-sufficient, independent children who will find jobs and spouses, and buy homes in which to live with their own nuclear families. Independence is less realistic today. The good news is that parents are much savvier, more aware and under-standing of the current struggles, making it more likely relatives can live together peacefully as adults. It's emotionally easier for today's twenty-somethings to live with their parents than it was in the 1960s and 1970s, because the generation gap is so much less divisive.

Sons and daughters admire the generation of parents who fought as feminists, who won rights for women, who forged on so women could work *and* raise children. It has become the norm for women in the workforce to have babies. Both those who stood up for these rights and those who benefited are accepted without question for the roles they have chosen. Parents take pride in their daughters' accomplishments and stand in awe of how much they've achieved. In so many ways, we've become a mutual admiration society, with less likelihood of being at odds when living together as grown-ups. And, single mothers, once questioned or demonized for their choices, today often command respect. In today's world, old models and presumptions carry little credence for parents or offspring.

ALL TOGETHER NOW

Long gone are the housedresses, bathrobes, and sedentary lifestyles that characterized generations past. Older genera-tions are healthier and more active than ever before. Inactivity among our elders has been replaced with exercise and youth-ful attitudes. It's common for grandparents today to feel like they are thirty-five rather than fifty or sixty. Eighty-year-olds run marathons and play singles tennis. Seniors take care of themselves so their children won't have to. Because of longer life expectancies and more openness to what younger generations believe, parents, like the returning college graduate, are welcomed by sons and daughters, daughters- and sons-in-law, and more-distant relatives. Living together again may seem unique or anxiety-producing to you, but it won't for long.

Within most families, fierce loyalty and interdependence prevail, and with that comes the feeling of wanting to help. On the flip side is the desire to be free of demands—children, to be free of their parents' needs, and parents, to be free of their children's needs. A parent may ask, "How did you get yourself into this mess?" or an adult child may say to his parent, "You need to make new friends, and have a life that doesn't include us all the time." Despite this, you will be at the ready to do whatever it takes to aid one another. Under the best of circumstances, having a stable career and family life is a challenge. Remember: No one loves and cares about you more than your family. They may groan or voice objections, but deep down, you're wanted.

Within most families, fierce loyalty and interdependence prevail, and with that comes the feeling of wanting to help.

Sure, there are all kinds of potential complications from too-tight quarters and emotional minefields, newly created and leftover from years ago, but these pages will help you sort through the various difficulties and give you ways to deal with or stop them. You will read about thoughts and feelings, along with advice and approaches to specific problems, from many perspectives. Each chapter opens with insights into what both a parent or an adult child may be thinking. They will give you greater insight and ideas to help you avoid possible misunderstandings and unpleasantness.

Will it be easy? Not all the time. Allow for mistakes, even heated discussions or explosions; expect someone to mess up now and again (and maybe it will be you). Nonetheless, years from now you'll look back and be happy for the time you had with your mother or father, your son or daughter, your brother or sister, or your nutty Aunt Bea. You will feel closer than ever, and be grateful for the security you provided, or had given to you when you needed it most.

You *can* go home again.

CHAPTER ONE

THE ART OF LIVING TOGETHER

REJOINING YOUR FAMILY MAY FEEL VERY FAMILIAR AND STRANGE at the same time. Odd for parents and grown children alike, because whether you are moving in with them or they with you, everyone's life will be somewhat different from what each has known. Odd, too, because you have been on your own perhaps for a very long time, doing what you pleased whenever you felt like it. That was then; this is now.

The idea that you have to put your life on hold to be accommodating or move just when you had most everything the way you wanted it can be disturbing and disruptive. Be it a permanent move or a short few month stopover, you'll be dealing with a son or daughter, a brother, sister, in-law, or parent's emotional baggage and belongings. Unsettling or somewhat different in the beginning, knowing what sets you or them off and having some solid strategies for coping will, in no time, have you wondering why you were worried. This book will help you create worry-free transitions and help you keep peace in your new blended household.

Families are coming together everywhere, often deciding to make living with family a first choice.

Families are coming together everywhere, often deciding to make living with family a first choice. Many adult children acknowledge that they knew their parents would live with them someday;

they just didn't think the day would be so soon. Several adult children told me that they bought their childhood homes in order to live with their parents. Others I spoke with have had a parent or in-law on the premises full-time for ten, twenty, even thirty years. College students and young families in increasing numbers conclude that returning home makes inordinate good sense. Rebecca, twenty-eight, frames her return home this way: "I assumed I would go home after college and find a job. I didn't have money to get a place of my own, and I know I can stay as long as I want. Besides, my parents are fun. The benefits outweigh any struggles as far as I'm concerned."

Rebecca's parents are most concerned about when she might leave. "Rebecca is so helpful and easy to be with, like having a good friend around all the time. I know she will move on eventually and we will miss her more than I want to think about now," says her mother.

There are valid reasons why living with nuclear family as adults happens so frequently, and in all different age groups. For one, society has given living with family again the thumbs-up; the shame and much of the hesitancy that once accompanied such moves have disappeared. Fueling the trend, too, is the realization that with your family, you have a support system unlike any you could get elsewhere. A friend will give you a couch or an extra room for a while, but that's tenuous at best. Perhaps you agree to shop and cook dinner for your roommate but you forget, and go out with another friend instead. One slipup like that on your part—you drink the beer he's cooling in the refrigerator or borrow a roommate's favorite purple sweater without asking—and you could be out the door. Family members, while not always enamored with your lapses, are

used to your quirky nature and know your unpleasant habits
. . . and you know theirs.

You can't be fired (at least, it's highly unlikely) from your job
as grandparent, parent, son, daughter, sister or brother, son- or
daughter-in-law. One of them may be there for you when you
never expected it, or thought you would need help, or have to
give it in such an all-encompassing way. You may love them fero-
ciously, feel lukewarm about them, or have a history of conflict;
nonetheless, most relatives are unconditional resources.

Husband or wife might not feel good about leaving a parent alone, or watching their young or middle-age adult child
grapple with credit card debt or child-care responsibilities and
expenses. If you're divorcing, it's better to go home than to
continue to live together miserably until you can afford separate places. Better to be with a relative who loves you and who
will look after your children when you can't.

Think of the family you'll be living with as your personal
EMT squad, even if it is not a dire emergency. How would you
treat those who rush in to give you emergency medical care?
Wouldn't you be appreciative? Give them the space and time
to help you? Not take advantage of the services they offer? Your
response: "Yes," to all questions, of course.

MOVING IN OR JUST VISITING?

As jobs dry up and companies clean house or freeze hiring,
young and old must amend their career directions. When these
scenarios are coupled with marital breakups or the death of a
parent, many find themselves seeking out their family of origin
as a lifeboat they can climb into to wait out the storm.

> ## What Your Parent May Be Thinking:
>
> *"My daughter and her husband planned to stay for a few weeks after her third child was born, and while renovating their house to make it larger. Problems with the zoning board and getting loans halted progress. Her two-year-old twin girls have taken over the house and my daughter has returned to work. I cook, clean, and do the laundry for all seven of us. I'm seventy-six, and not sure how long I can keep up this pace. Then I think, What will we do when they leave?"*
>
> Ruth and her eighty-year-old husband are in the second year of sharing their home.

In this new era, grandma Ruth turns her life over to her daughter and grandchildren; Ian's parents provide assistance on a continuing basis; and the many families like them prolong their togetherness. When Ian asked if he could move home for two weeks until he found someone with whom to share an apartment, his parents agreed. Five years later, his mother is conflicted: While quick to divulge that she finds her son's inability to get on with his life frustrating, she adores having him around. "I love having Ian home; he's so up on what's going on. He can fix anything, and he's a great chef. It's like having Bobby Flay at the grill in my backyard," his mother says. She is like so many parents who see the upside and try to overlook the areas they find troublesome, like their child not hustling enough to find work, or feeling that staying

What Your Adult Child May Be Thinking:

"My first concern was, Would they take me back? I'm the oldest child, and they had just sent the youngest off to college. I was thinking, They're finally free and then one of us comes back, so they might not want me."

Ian, thirty-three, moved home five years ago when his company downsized and he couldn't pay his rent.

home too long stunts an adult child's development or inhibits his social life.

The "me-first" attitude that infiltrated the last couple of generations is dissipating, particularly when it comes to family. More and more people have begun to rethink what they believe constitutes family, and the hopes they have for their own. In part because of the economic conditions, our renewed sense of family unity has begun to resemble Chinese Americans and others groups with strong ties to their cultures—cultures that value and identify with the traditions of obligation, assistance, and support.

The "me-first" attitude that infiltrated the last couple of generations is dissipating, particularly when it comes to family.

William Poy Lee, author of *The Eighth Promise: An American Son Pays Tribute to His Toisanese Mother*, says "Chinese Americans of all ages, while rejecting the idea that they are bound by obligation to live with or care for parents as they age, have returned to a notion of filial piety reinvigorated by core American values of equality, individual freedom and choice." Lee's youngest brother, when in his early thirties, chose to live with their mother—not because he assumed the ancient Chinese guiding principle, but because "as Mom became less physically able, he wanted to reciprocate the care she provided him as a child," adds Lee.

In the midst of the 2008–2009 recession, *Time* magazine flagged one cover story with the message, "The recession has changed more than just how we live. It's changed what we value and what we expect—even after the economy recovers." Although the article focused on frugality, the concept is equally apropos of renewed family ideals, emphasizing solidarity and support for relatives who need it.

Freelance journalist Caitlin Shetterly and her husband, Daniel Davis, a freelance commercial photographer, returned home to Maine from California when they could not afford their rent. Hers is a story like so many, of recession and job losses and being able to return to family who loves her with a husband, dog, and baby. After a ten-day drive across the country, Caitlin's father greeted them in his driveway. His welcome, reported to NPR by Caitlin, reflects how many parents feel when their adult children come home. "It's so wonderful to see you here. I mean, I know what you've been through and just how difficult everything's been, but what an incredible upside to all these trials, having you home. Whatever comes next, this is the best."

RELUCTANT RESIDENTS

If you're reading this book, you probably have a family that wants you no matter what. So many people have no one to count on when bogged down in debt or entangled in a nasty divorce. Feel lucky. Your parents don't have to let you move in, and you don't have to let parents, in-laws, siblings, or grown children live with you. That's the bottom line. You want it to work, and so do the people you're living with . . . and it will.

Olivia had no qualms about returning home at age thirty. "Moving back for me wasn't a thought process. I had lived there summers and knew it would work out. My sister, her husband, and new baby are struggling to make ends meet, *That's the bottom line. You want it to work, and so do the people you're living with . . . and it will.* and I keep telling them to come home. It's the best place to be when your life isn't going well or it's not where you want it to be.

"My parents would love it if my sister lived with us, especially my mother. And, a grandchild to boot! My mother might quit her job. She's an over-nurturing nurturer. The more people around, the better she likes it . . . and she can't do enough for whoever is in the house."

Could be you are ready and delighted with the prospect of moving back or having a relative move in with you. Or, like Olivia's sister, you're holding out, not wanting to return home. Olivia's sister is praying for a job to come through that will allow her family to keep their house and their friends, and avoid a move to a destination where they will, in many ways, have to start over.

There are no statistics or studies on how many people move in with relatives happily and how many move in reluctantly. Regardless of how you came to be living with your family again, you may be reticent about what seems a forced turn of events—a step backward in your path or life's direction.

Reluctant residents in your house, or you in theirs, encompass a wide spectrum of discontent. Those who are "hosting" should understand that any lack of enthusiasm is not necessarily about them. In so many instances and at any age, it can feel like a trap for adult children returning to the city or town they grew up in. A return to a hometown they believed was stifling or limiting is the bigger issue. Others are unhappy with the way their lives have veered off course, causing them to be treading in what they perceive to be perilous waters.

Attitudes, of course, depend on individual situations which can change over time. John, forty-two, is married with two children, and lost his job as an engineer in the auto industry. "We never expected to move back in with my parents. We didn't plan for it; we didn't want it," says John. The move had many pluses, but in the beginning John had tunnel vision when it came to the negatives. His nine- and eleven-year-old daughters shared a room for the first time and he worried they would argue more than they already did. At first the girls suffered academically in a new school, and were slow to make new friends. On the upside, the children saw their grandparents every day versus every few months. Once his daughters had acclimated (as children tend to do), John was able to recognize how fortunate he was to have his parents' support.

Although Kimberly chose to live with her father, it isn't exactly where she saw herself in her mid-forties, proving again that circumstances often get in the way of our plans and dreams. "This isn't the way I wanted my life to be. I saw myself with a husband and four children at this point. I can't tell you how many times a week I ask myself, 'Where is my husband and where are my children?'" laments Kimberly. Then she pivots to put a positive spin on her current living arrangement with her dad. "I'm so glad my father is alive and we have each other. The husband? For now I have to live my life without him." She's making the best of it.

Formerly self-sufficient parents who move in with their adult children also have a tough time accepting their dependence, as do young adults who sense their privacy has been stripped and their privileges curtailed. Others feel as if they are not carrying their weight. Jeremy Diamond, a 2009 New Jersey college graduate, is ready to take responsibility for himself, but could not land a job after sending out a seemingly endless number of résumés. He told the *New York Times,* "My parents give me everything, but I don't want to put more strain on them. I should be handling my own stuff."

Whatever the reason you're boomeranging, it's unlikely that it's entirely your fault—so stop blaming yourself.

Whether it happens at age twenty-two or fifty-two, a fervent job hunt that turns up empty damages pride and gnaws at self-esteem. Relatives can be just the booster you need to cope with any anger and disappointment you feel, as well as a huge help assisting you in putting together the pieces of your life puzzle. Whatever the reason you're boomeranging, it's unlikely that it's entirely your fault—so stop blaming yourself. Those you live with should take into account your reservations, regret, or sadness, because these feelings affect how the family functions as a unit.

THE FAMILY SYSTEM

Under optimal circumstances, both parties see the move as positive. Living together is not being forced on either of you, and you want to get along. And yet, as much as family is a safety net, it is also a net that can get unmercifully tangled if you don't handle it carefully.

When the children were growing up, each member of the family had roles, some defined by age, birth order, or family needs. As adults, those roles are likely to shift somewhat or be reassigned. The changes affect how the people within the family relate to one another. It doesn't make a difference how well you got along with your parents, your children, or your siblings when you lived together years or decades ago; the relationships will require some modification if they are to work now that you are all adults.

Just like adding a new baby to the family causes upheaval in each relationship, the dynamics of how everyone interacts and spends time together will be different. Having an adult child come home, for example, can become a balm for the parents' marriage or a wedge, providing constant fodder for disagreement. In Marilyn's opinion, her son at age forty has overstayed his welcome. "I disagree with my husband about what our son could do to make his life better. What I dislike the most is the strain the situation puts on our marriage."

Adult child Sophia, thirty-six, believes that she helped her mother and stepfather's relationship. "I kept the balance in the house. My stepfather is too strong for my mom. She can't stand up to him, but comments from me that changed a discussion helped to smooth out their relationship and avoid outbursts."

Relationships you thought were rock-solid, like those with your grandchildren, can take a different spin when they are an integral part of your life. "When my daughter and grandchildren visited, they got whatever they wanted because it wasn't an everyday event," says Carmen, a fifty-nine-year-old grandmother. Her two grandchildren moved to her home with their mother five years ago, when the children were ages six and eight. "Living with them, I find I'm constantly disciplining. I have lots of rules and like order, which didn't matter so much when I saw them occasionally. You want to wake up and have good times with your grandchildren, but that's not happening now that we live together."

SIBLINGS WITH AND WITHOUT ATTITUDE

Siblings can be overjoyed that you are living with their parent. They are thrilled that he or she is not alone, or relieved that they don't have to contend with all the headaches that come with having a difficult parent. "My siblings are incredulous that I moved in with our parents," says Monica, fifty-six. "They have their own lives and are amazed. Nothing more."

In other families, the juggling of relationships touches sensitive chords and elicits subtle—or, at other times, obvious—objections to the close relationship that develops when parents and one brother or sister share a home. You may have a pesky younger sibling who still lives at home, maybe in your former room, which you want back and he refuses to vacate. He had your parents to himself, and now his older sibling is barging into his territory and occupying his parents' thoughts and some of their time. Little brother is not into sharing, and shows it in every possible way.

After living at home for a few years, you and your mother have developed an ease in the kitchen; the two of you glide seamlessly through meal preparation. Where both you and your sister once helped with the cooking, your sister makes herself scarce whenever she visits. She's adept at cooking for her husband and children; you're pretty sure your sister thinks you've won over your mother in all things culinary, but she would never say so.

Siblings may likewise be jealous when parents support one child, in their view, "excessively," or when one sibling fulfills the lion's share of their parents' needs. A brother might make direct reference to his resentment by asking a parent, "How can you let my sister use you like this?" or "She's taking advantage of you." Parents can refuse to get into the conversation. Another solution is to do what Wendy, whose oldest son lives with her and her husband, did when her other children confronted her. She said, "I would do the same for you. If you have a better way, I will listen. Tell me." She will not put her son on the street. In her mind's eye, she says, "If I do, I see him pushing a shopping cart overflowing with his possessions. I can't do that." Most parents can't.

Siblings who cannot comprehend how another can move in are, for the most part, in secure marital and/or financial positions that make it easy to be judgmental. Nicole, twenty-nine, is married to a man who has three younger siblings. "They express their disapproval openly," Nicole states. "They think we are taking advantage because we had a second child while living with my in-laws. They tell my husband, 'You are the oldest, and you're growing your family in Mom and Dad's house. You shouldn't be doing that.'"

Brothers and sisters can lose their high regard for each other when a sibling is down on his luck and forced to move home. Sophia feels the effects of what she refers to as her downward spiral when health issues and divorce at age thirty-six necessitated her move home. "I'm the oldest child in the family. My brothers used to look up to me and call me for advice. They've lost all respect for me, and that hurts. I can't wait to get my life together again."

Siblings not living in the same household may feel left out or fear that you are taking financial advantage. "People get funny about money," says Dawn, forty, who lives with her two children and mother. "My mother has money, and I don't want my sister and brother to think I'm spending all of it

Siblings not living in the same household may feel left out or fear that you are taking financial advantage.

on me or my children. I keep very careful records of who paid for what."

When you live with older parents, your siblings may, frankly, worry about getting a fair share of the inheritance if there is money to bequeath. There's a lot to contend with and overcome emotionally, even without the pressures of what amounts to basic sibling rivalry in its many forms.

TOGETHER AGAIN—THE CHALLENGE

There are adults of all ages who fold back into their family of origin like a hot air balloon gliding to earth—softly, without a hitch, and without upsetting other offspring or relatives, parents, or themselves. More common and problematic are family members who bounce between their old and new roles. Central to the core of adult children and parents living together, however, is the challenge to ease off on parenting. As author Adele Faber so aptly points out, "[T]he desire to be needed is very powerful in parents. To go from that all-powerful parent whose kids desperately need you to someone who sees a child as a separate individual is a very hard journey." For many parents this is a critical process that must be mastered if they hope to live amicably as adults in the same house with their grown children.

To smooth the course, parents will have to make concessions—some minor, some major. To hold up their end, adult children who return home will have to find ways to be helpful and show their appreciation, as will in-laws and parents who settle into their adult children's homes. Focusing on the positives and pitching in wherever possible will help ensure that living together again will have fewer potholes.

You can also expect some contention stemming from generational differences. You may argue about what music to play or what television programs to watch. You're a spender; your parent, a saver. There may be conflict in the child-rearing arena, or between mother-in-law and son- or daughter-in-law regarding just about anything. You may consider your daughter-in-law a know-it-all, or your son or son-in-law unmotivated. Or you may see your mother- or father-in-law as overly critical or meddling. How will you live with these feelings, and this person?

Every family has unique issues that make life as an adult nuclear family interesting, and at times taxing. Interacting with parents, relatives, and grown-up children is a balancing act which requires special insights. For that reason alone, as you read, you'll begin to understand your counterpart's thinking and find the words or actions to reach a compromise. This book will provide tools to help you adjust your approach and to overcome most problems that arise.

Interacting with parents, relatives, and grown-up children is a balancing act which requires special insights.

Wherever you land, and with whichever family member, whether it's a permanent move or a transitional stop, whether you chose the move or it was the result of circumstances you had little control over, you can remain in charge of yourself. Expect good days and bad, ups and downs, for you personally as well as for the people you live with. At age thirty, Eric moved back home after graduate school and a stint on his own. He didn't want to throw money away on rent, and his parents live where he wants to be (New York) for the next two or three years. "Having moved out and coming back, I appreciate my parents' company. My mom says 'Maybe you should stay here until we die.' It's a great place to live, and there's no reason to leave. When she's in a good mood, she wants me forever. When she's having a bad day, she wants me out. You can always tell what my mom is thinking."

ATTITUDES THAT MAKE LIVING TOGETHER EASIER

Families and individual needs are complicated; there's no one answer that works for everyone. Here are some attitudes to adopt to assist you in meeting most obstacles in your own situation. With these recommendations in mind, you'll be able to work around the difficulties, and reap rewards you weren't expecting.

- Appreciate that you have a place to live with people who love you.
- Understand that you will have to be flexible.
- Be ready to compromise.
- Stop thinking that you failed as a parent, or as a person.
- Give up the guilt.
- Accept that your life will change.
- Make a pact with yourself to give the living arrangement a few months; don't expect it to work perfectly right away.

Chapter Two

Establishing Boundaries

THE CLOSENESS YOU HAD WHEN YOU LIVED TOGETHER AS PARENT and child was vital for you both then. When living separate lives you most likely found a comfort zone in which you erected personal boundaries that afforded you time to yourself and the freedom to live as you wished. Boundaries separating you from family occur automatically when you're independent, formed either by the physical distance or the amount of contact you orchestrate.

When you live together again, those lines can blur rapidly. If boundaries go undrawn and unchecked, one or the other of you may feel smothered—like the child you once were, or the supervising parent you no longer want to be. In this chapter you will learn how to set important ground rules that will help reestablish and guard the boundaries you had when you lived on your own.

As you settle in the same house, decades-old problems may take new forms, ones instantly identifiable because parents lapse into seeing their offspring as they were during their formative years. If your teen "screwed up" then, you're likely to be waiting for and expecting a repeat. But, this isn't the same rebellious, perhaps a trifle inconsiderate, teenager who left years ago. Although returning offspring will rely on their parents to some degree, they should be viewed as independent adults, even when parents' emotional or financial support is required.

As a full-time mother, perhaps you were a bit intrusive. What makes you think you will stay out of your adult child's life now? Similarly, as the grown-up child, you may still see your parents or siblings through your young person's prism—when your parents inserted themselves into aspects of your life you preferred to keep to yourself, or when your sister, always the free spirit, did what she pleased, including reading your diary and borrowing your clothes (or your boyfriend). You worry that they will not necessarily respect you or your belongings all these years later. As adults, we all need more private, emotional space as protection against the intrusion of others.

As much as some things stay the same, others change, so even if you got along growing up, you're bound to run into a few difficulties. Realizing that everyone will have to make modifications and concessions will help you reframe your attitude and be more accepting of what has to change.

In the extreme, Barbara's mother is an uneasy driver, and refuses to make left-hand turns. She doesn't want her fifty-one-year-old daughter to make them either. She worked out right-hand-turn-only routes to the supermarket, beauty salon, and bank—virtually every place she and her daughter routinely drive. When behind the wheel, rather than distress her mother, Barbara concedes and follows these circuitous trails for reasons she can't explain.

As you tackle the problems of establishing firm boundaries, it's important to stay flexible. Sometimes roles shift and boundary lines change in the process. Don't be surprised if there's a reversal of roles. As the adult child, you may find yourself the organizer, running the household. Once your parent cooked dinner every night; ***Don't be surprised*** now you're at the stove. A parent ***if there's a reversal*** soothed your teenage hysteria, but ***of roles.*** now you're the soothing influence for your single, dating mother. When you lived together as parent and child, you sought your parent's advice, but now a parent seeks yours . . . and follows it. But, is this neediness absorbing all your time and energy?

If you've just moved in, or your adult child is about to, consider that she might want to hold on to her independent adult status and privacy. Parents, on the other hand, might be assessing how much independence they are losing, or how their office now has to revert back to a son or daughter's bedroom. Each of you will devise better ways of dealing with your own or your family's behaviors and reactions that interfere with one another's personal life.

WHOLE LOT OF CHANGING GOING ON

Living with other adults is a time to initiate change in how you think about a particular situation and how it impacts you and the people you live with. Through this exercise, you can protect yourself, avoid stepping on each other's toes, and prevent sacrificing most, if not all, your time and emotional space.

If you've lived on your own for a while and got used to not having to report in, alerting those you live with to your schedule will be an adjustment. It may feel as if you've gained a permanent monitor. A young adult living at home again with no siblings in the house, for example, will have all the attention on

---

What Your Parent May Be Thinking:

"I had some reservations about living with my daughter again. As a teenager, she and I had had issues. I realized that both of us would have to make some adjustments. She feels I should be more outgoing and active, that I should not climb into bed at 7:00 p.m. with a book or watch TV until I fall asleep or hibernate in my warm bed for much of the day in winter."

Helen, eighty-three, lives with her daughter whose three adult children live independently in different states.

---

her. She can't slip under the radar; her comings and goings will be known, and everything she does will get noticed.

But on the other hand, you now have someone who worries about where you are—someone who cares if you come home at night. Pamela, whose mother moved in with her when

---

What Your Adult Child May Be Thinking:

"I forget that I can't wait until the next day to clean up after my friends, and that I can't leave my shoes by the front door. It's annoying to be told to take care of your shoes, but after growing up with my mother, I know this. I have to respect her ways and take care of my things right away. My parents are helping me out by letting me live with them."

Adam, twenty-seven, returned home to get his debt under control.

Pamela was in her mid-fifties, is convinced her loss of privacy is a trade-off that's well worth it. "I live in a major city and believe there's safety in numbers. I find it comforting to have someone waiting for me who cares that I come home."

Adult children worry about their parents, too, as Sarah, twenty-five, who lives home, admits: "When my parents are away and I don't hear from them, I imagine something has happened." *Worrying about someone you love, whatever their age, is universal.* Worrying about someone you love, whatever their age, is universal. "Out of sight, out of mind" works, but as soon as the person is in range, the worrying starts. Go easy on the worried parent or adult child, and adopt solutions to reduce that concern.

To signal your safe return home, you might turn off a light your parent leaves on. On waking in the middle of the night to darkness, your parent will turn over and go back to sleep. You might agree to call at any hour if you decide you won't be in until morning. These simple courtesies help to reduce anxiety, and for some, like Sarah, the guilt. "I tend to forget to let my parents know when I won't be home. The worst part is if my mother doesn't ring my cell phone to find out where I am, but tells me the next day she was up all night, 'worried sick.' I recognize the consequences of my actions and feel terrible. It's not worth the guilt."

You might try to convince the worriers in your house to ascribe to the mind-set that bad news travels fast: If something is wrong, they will know soon enough. If having to report in bothers you or ups your guilt level:

You Might Say: How old am I? Or, you're behaving like my parent.

Your Parent or Adult Child Might Say: "I don't care; age isn't the issue. I worry when I don't know where you are or when to expect you."

Compromise Options: "I will call if I am going to be later than usual, or later than the time I said I'd be home." Or, "If you don't hear from me by xxx time, call me. I may have gotten involved and forgotten to call."

PUTTING GROUND RULES IN PLACE

One of the first orders of business is to install ground rules that reshuffle the boundaries to ensure everyone's freedom and independence. Conversations around keeping track of where-abouts, privacy, food preferences, punctuality, and personal time are good ones to have as soon as you start living together again, or as soon as one of them becomes an issue or irritant. If you want rules, make them clear, but not in an authoritative way—more in the manner you would tell your husband or wife, "I know you need to know this."

In a solid marriage, you have agreed-upon obligations and routines: who empties the dishwasher, who drives the kids to soccer practice, who starts dinner, who takes out the garbage, who wakes up whom at 7:30 a.m., ideally handing over a cup of freshly brewed coffee. The marriage glides along relatively smoothly until one of the routines or an agreement is broken.

When a family member or you arrive, you have no real rules in place. Even though you grew up with the same people you live with, and remember "the rules," they will have to be somewhat different now. In the years you were apart, much will have changed in terms of what you need to be happy. Unstated policies or wishes create an unnecessary undercurrent of tension.

Ground Rule #1: Being Considerate

When you lived alone or with a partner in your own space, for the sake of argument, everything had its proper place and you had responsibilities and ways of doing things. For instance, you liked the fact that when you put the sugar away, it was right where you left it the next time you needed it. Coats were hung up when you walked in the door, never left thrown over the closest chair. If you bought ice cream and, after a few spoonfuls, you stored the carton in the back of the freezer, it would still be there, ready for your next craving.

A son-in-law, daughter, brother, or grandchildren have joined your household. Sweaters, jackets, and toys litter the floor; the sugar is somewhere you would never dream of putting it; and the ice cream you were hoarding—well, the carton is in the freezer, but there's only half a teaspoon left. And sometimes the carton sits empty on the kitchen counter with a sticky spoon next to it. You need to come to some sort of understanding.

Lack of consideration and disarray bother a lot of people, and can become bones of contention.

Lack of consideration and disarray bother a lot of people, and can become bones of contention, usually more for one party than the other. Typically, mothers who have their adult children back home react with horror at the heaps of clothing, half-empty glasses, unmade beds, and piles of "stuff" everywhere. They wonder how a child of theirs could have gone so far "downhill" in the years they lived away from them.

Seems petty, but if you're a parent who likes the beds made by 8:00 a.m. (or just made at some point) and now live with an adult child who believes making the bed is a waste of time, let the other person know the unmade bed goes against your "tidy" way of being.

You Might Say: "I care how my home looks, and the unmade bed annoys me."

Your Grown Child Might Say: "That's silly. No one looks at it . . . whoever goes near my room?"

Compromise Options: Agree to make the bed. Agree to keep your door closed if the bed is unmade. Allow your parent in your room to make the bed as she wishes.

Ann, fifty-eight, chose the first of the three compromise options, to no avail. "My efforts at hospital corners go unnoticed. My mother remakes the bed at some point during the day—and that's fine with me."

When young grandchildren move in with their grandparents, they can literally take over the house, as happened to seventy-six-year-old Margery. When she raised her children she was very particular; nothing was out of place. "I'm more relaxed now. Having a neat house isn't as important as it was when I was younger. The children's toys stay wherever they leave them, and I'm okay with that."

Both Ann and Margery pick their battles wisely and conclude that confrontation over orderliness and neatness isn't worth the effort. They changed their way of thinking to eliminate entanglements over what they decided wasn't all that important.

Being considerate can be contagious. Sometimes if you help one person, the other person figures out that he has to help. If you are sharing cars, for instance, and your parent inconveniences herself so you can have the car one day, you remember her generosity the next time she needs the car. In this way, a whole scheme of cooperating evolves within the family.

Ground Rule # 2: Protecting Your Privacy

Bedroom privacy, once defined, draws a crucial boundary line for the living arrangement. Be you the parent or the adult child, you can make your room strictly off-limits for any reason, particularly to maintain privacy. It's hard to believe, but there are parents of twenty- and thirty-somethings who enter their offspring's bedrooms without warning, as if the occupant were still in grade school. Even if there's no one visiting, it is a gross invasion of privacy to enter a room with a closed door without knocking.

Bedroom privacy, once defined, draws a crucial boundary line for the living arrangement.

At different times in her adult life, Alice, thirty-five, returned to live with each of her parents, who divorced when she was nine years old. "They both barged in; my mom at midnight when I was on the phone with my boyfriend. And, my dad . . . I was shocked. It was around 10:00 p.m. I could have been undressed. It was completely unacceptable, and I told him. 'I'm an adult; you can't just walk in whenever you feel like it.' I was pretty upset both times, and my parents realized that they had to warn me . . . they had to yell to me, or certainly knock. Yes, they own their homes, but it is my room, if only temporarily."

Too often it's the lack of consideration or small inconveniences that start a fight or are viewed as infractions of guidelines that were assumed, but never verbalized. They can catch you completely off guard. Stephanie, thirty-one, found her mother outside the bathroom screaming at 7:00 a.m., "Get out of the shower! What do you think you're doing, hogging the bathroom like that? I have to get ready for work, too." Stephanie felt her mother's yelling was unreasonable since her mother rises at least an hour earlier than she does on weekdays. Stephanie decided that a yelling match early in the morning was no way to begin the day; they needed to establish ground rules around bathroom use.

You Might Say: "Mother, we have to talk about this. I take a shower at this time every single morning, and have for months."

Your Parent Might Say: "What's to talk about? It's my house. If I sleep late, I want the bathroom when I want it."

Compromise Options: Set a time frame for each person to shower in the morning. Or, one might shower at night. Or, there may be an understanding that Stephanie will be out of the shower by xxx time on workdays to prevent future early-morning assaults.

Ground Rule # 3: Sticking to Food Preferences

Establishing boundaries may include what's in the cupboard and put on the table. For those who are dieting or with strong preferences or nutritional needs, you will want to discuss the matter, or decide you can live with someone else's choices.

Marilyn and her daughter and son don't share the same palate—not even close. Meals are truly a case of "separate tables" in her home. Marilyn prepares dinner for her husband, while her offspring makes their own; one leans toward frozen dinners, the other is a strict vegetarian. Once they resolved as a family that the "children" would pay for and prepare their own food, the tension around who was eating what stopped.

Establishing boundaries may include what's in the cupboard and put on the table.

If you watch your weight and live with a parent who doesn't, it can be discouraging to have a mother or father who stocks the house with everything you love, but have no willpower to resist. One way to handle the problem is to prepare the shopping list together and veto those items that tempt you. But even that can backfire. Jacqui and her mother-in-law agreed to write up weekly meal plans and sensible shopping lists. She reports on a recent outcome: "Last shopping day we got a bag of apples. When I got home from work the next day, I was greeted by my mother-in-law, holding a platter of warm apple turnovers. I protested and was told, 'I don't like naked apples.' " Resolute, Jacqui adds, "I'm going to have to live with homemade treats and save my energy for important issues."

If you are on a low-salt diet yourself, and your son or daughter-in-law does most of the cooking, you can't ignore their heavy hand with the saltshaker. When it's a matter of your health, you'll want to firmly state your dietary restrictions.

Ground Rule # 4: Respecting Others' Time

If you are the type about whom people say they can set their watches, few things are more displeasing than waiting for people who are chronically late. You are super punctual, and your anxiety level soars if you think you will be late; your parent or adult child, on the other hand, believes being on time or early for appointments is senseless. They argue that meetings never begin when they are supposed to, and carry that philosophy over into family interactions.

If tardiness unhinges you, you will want to try to rectify the situation with the "resident" who is regularly late for dinner, late for work, late for the movies—late for whatever you plan to do together.

The Chronically Tardy Might Say: "I get there, don't I? Why are you so agitated? It's just the family. Relax."

You Might Say: "It's inconsiderate and rude. Being late makes me anxious (or, more strongly, it ruins the occasion for me). Please allow more time in the future."

Compromise Options:

- Give the tardy person a fifteen-minute grace period by slicing those minutes off the actual arrival time.

- Or, give a warning: "We will go ahead without you (and leave a note where to meet you), or we will eat dinner without you."

- Let latecomers know you will not make excuses for them.

- Trust that the other person's tardiness is not a reflection on you and live with it.

Drastic measures: Stop including the chronically late in time-sensitive plans.

Ground Rule # 5: Protecting Your Time

Most boundary issues are reconcilable. A few—like how much time you devote to the people you live with—are more delicate to resolve. As adults, you all have a say in when and how much time is given over to your parent, adult child, sibling, aunt, or uncle. Most people want more time and space, and feel trapped by practical and emotional drains that leave no time for anything beyond family.

SOLVING TIME-EATING DILEMMAS

Dilemma #1: One or the other of you may be a master at getting someone to take care of your business—be it making plane reservations, scheduling doctor appointments, or getting the car repaired. Pull back; the needy person will begin to take some initiative and you'll be off the hook.

Dilemma #2: You may have a reputation for being the "responsible" one, but that can change. Limit time-eating chores another person can execute, and stop being the personal assistant to your parent or adult child. You cannot force someone to tend to their own assorted tasks, but you can remind

TIME-PROTECTION OPTIONS

For those who would monopolize you, these time-protection options help reaffirm that you are not abandoning the home front, *and* will allow the other person to adjust his or her level of neediness and dependency to your availability.

- Figure out if the desire to be together or compunction to be accessible is a problem—and whose it is.
- Refuse to tend to time-eating tasks the other person should be able to execute on his own.
- Assess if giving in to family wishes will curtail your freedom significantly.
- Go over your schedule to demonstrate how restricted your time is.
- Although you don't have a lot of free time for your parent or adult child, explain that you love him or her, regardless.
- Determine the time you want to devote to family so that it doesn't disrupt your life and giving it doesn't pressure you.

them that you are unavailable. Make recommendations on how to accomplish whatever needs doing.

Dilemma #3: One of you is a caregiver in the extreme. The perpetual desire—or compulsion—to care for your relative is unhealthy for the relationship. Such behavior feeds emotional dependency and swallows up free time.

Dilemma #4: Before living together, you were super connected to your parents or adult child via cell phone and text messages. You may feel differently now about sharing the intimate details of your life, and you may want more separation. Constant calls and messages interrupt, distract, and result in poor use of time. Turn off your cell phone or online e-mail; screen your calls; and stop responding to every text or instant message. What someone has to tell or ask you can usually wait a bit.

If you allow yourself to become overly mired in family obligations, it's easy to forget that you have a life, too. Whether you're the adult child, parent, grandparent, or sibling in all this, you are likely to be happier when you keep your boundaries sharply delineated and secure. And, when people in your family overstep these boundaries, be sure to let them know. Doing so ensures your ability to come and go freely, to be with friends, and to maintain a separate life.

Chapter Three

Great (and Not so Great) Expectations

Everyone—parents, adult children, siblings—has memories of the years they lived together, some divine, some distasteful. Those recollections will flavor how you feel about living under the same roof again. If you grew up with a parent who secretly listened to your phone conversations, combed your room for signs of drugs, or looked through your high school test papers, you will be concerned about how much privacy you'll have.

As parents, if your son or daughter was a teenage procrastinator, you are most likely expecting more of the same. Raised an inflexible child? You will worry that the stubbornness will resurface to make your life difficult when you move in with her or she with you. Or, you might be put off by your adult child's dependence on you and fear it will be worse when the two of you have daily interaction again.

The aim is to develop realistic expectations of living together. You will discover that knowing how to understand the person (or people) you live with, evaluating and expressing your expectations—and sometimes lowering them—can help avoid disappointment and discord.

Perhaps a long-ago volatile difference of opinion will color your attitude all these years later. What you remember from the past and what you hope to attain together become expectations for what life will be like in the "new regime." A good rule of thumb to follow, however, is: Don't expect more from your

---

What Your Parent May Be Thinking:

"When he was younger, I couldn't wait to get rid of him. I had fantasies about changing the locks on my doors. He was quite difficult, often explosive and angry. His talent was taking any set of circumstances and turning it so I was the bad guy. I anticipated the old problems would resurface, but his behavior has so improved. He controls his temper and even capitulates. I will miss him when he leaves."

Suzanne is sixty-five, and has been living with her twenty-nine-year-old son for four years.

---

parents than you had growing up. If your mother was distant the whole time you were a child, absorbed by her job, and is now moving in as a grandparent to help you with your children, you need to ask her outright what she's willing to do. What can you count on her to handle? Similarly, don't expect more responsibility from your grown child simply because he has been out in the world for a few years (or decades). That said, you may be pleasantly surprised.

What Your Adult Child May Be Thinking:

"As a child and teenager, I never knew when my mother would lose it and rant at me. She was pretty scary when she was angry. I was hoping she would be different, but the smallest things still set her off."

Devan, twenty-seven, returned home two years ago after losing her job.

REMEMBRANCE OF THINGS PAST

Looking back provides sound emotional preparation. If you got along well earlier in your life, the chances are much better that you will now. Elizabeth, eighty, told me about her two daughters, one easygoing, the other headstrong, from early ages. Clara, the elder daughter, remembers the smallest of slights dating back to her fourth birthday party. She refused to invite a close family friend's child because the youngster had opened one of her gifts the year before. "Clara and I would not do well living together; she doesn't let go of anything," her mother explained. In contrast, Diane, the younger, "doesn't hold a grudge. I can say what I want and she'll accept it. In the past, when we've argued, it blows over quickly and we're friends again. We can live together and get along whatever comes up."

Looking back provides sound emotional preparation.

Even if you got along fabulously well with your parents as a teen, or as an adult while you lived in *your* own house, you may have doubts about sharing your parents' home with your spouse and children. Life together is immeasurably less turbulent for those who anticipate what may happen. The following questions are a good starting point to help you discern how you feel about the relatives with whom you will be living for the foreseeable future. Answers will also help you determine what in the relationship needs modification if you are all to be content.

Sorting Out Expectations

- As adults, has there been a balance of give and take?

- Will too much be expected of you?

- Will demands on your time be too great?

- Are you too easily influenced by a parent's or adult child's suggestions?

- Are you already overly involved in their lives, or they in yours?

- Do you have clearly defined boundaries?

- Do you respect each other?

- Are you made to feel guilty?

- Will you get what you need emotionally?

- Is there too much disagreement on issues both large and small?

However you answer these questions, know that the adjustment period may be awkward and difficult at first. Everyone should understand the reasons for living together again and be in agreement that this is the best route. Still, as a parent, you could be unhappy with your thirty-something daughter for her lack of direction or inability to save. And as an adult child, you could be displeased with yourself for having to rely on your parents or in-laws.

Those who have very positive expectations and the history on which to base them can also run into glitches. "My dad picked me up every Wednesday after school and took me for a special treat—an ice cream, a movie, visiting the bears at the zoo," explains Kimberly. When she moved in with her seventy-nine-year-old father a few years ago, her expectations, based on their decades-ago relationship, were high. Back in the same house, they learned that they didn't agree completely on finances or orderliness. Unanticipated hurdles in the relationship can be dodged when the family focuses on its expectations individually and jointly.

KNOWING THE PLAYERS

In any sport or game, understanding your teammates is critical to success—be it for the pure fun of it, or for winning. Who will pass the ball, who will sulk if he doesn't have the ball, who calls the plays, and what plays win the game are all crucial to success. As you take up residence with a relative again, acknowledging each "player's" style, strong points, and telltale signs of trouble or discontent provides essential clues that avert meltdowns and mishaps and make the time together a winning experience.

When you know, or think you know, what you've gotten yourself into, it's far easier to accept differences in style. "I'm a neatnik, but I am used to my daughter's messes and have decided that I can live with the jumble that surrounds her life." Elizabeth understands that she's not going to change that part of her fifty-year-old daughter's personality, and overlooks the disorder because they are compatible on other fronts.

In some families, maybe yours, conflict marks the tenor of the relationships for as long as you can remember. There are parents and adult children who were and remain personality mismatches; they never got along and still don't, but have no alternative but to live together. "My husband and daughter fight, my daughter threatens to leave, they apologize to each other, and all is well until the next disagreement," says Francine, whose daughter and three grandchildren have been living with them for a decade. "I try to stay out of it," she adds, "but often I feel like a referee."

When you don't have a family referee like Francine, or you aren't able to look the other way, be alert to the hazards that you know already exist or have the potential to cause tension: a parent who needs parenting; an adult child who needs to be the center of attention. Aware, you can be prepared to cope when a problem arises.

While you may be fearful of putting several strong personalities in the same house, your trepidation could turn out to be unfounded. Elaine worried when both of her children, now twenty-seven and thirty years old, came home after trying assorted living scenarios with and without partners. "I have a strong personality, and so do each of my children. They have a history of clashing with me, and like many siblings growing up, they fought relentlessly. I thought there would be a lot of drama again. As grown-ups they are wonderful together, and for me that negates a lot of the crap that went on when they were young. They were not fun. Turns out for the three of us, living together is golden. The spats stopped. We have all grown up."

GREAT EXPECTATIONS

If it's time to move in, it's time to move on and relearn how to make joining forces with family harmonious. Like anything new and different, it takes time to adjust. Be patient; the relationship will progress and improve as you get used to each other again. You'll want to talk about your expectations at the outset. Possible snags can be eased or prevented entirely by up-front conversation and a thoughtful look at what everyone thinks will happen.

Tackling the major issues—How long will you or they stay? Who contributes financially, and how much? Who does what to help out?—lets everyone know the parameters. Being open is also a good barometer of how well you will be able to communicate with each other going forward. You're not signing a contract; you're just laying the foundation.

An ambiguous time frame can test the relationship. When Ian, thirty-three, first arrived, his parents asked him how long he would be there. He had no idea because he didn't know when or if his once full-time job might resume. He couldn't afford an apartment on the freelance hours he was working. He made up a departure date. *A plan is useless if you don't revisit it now and then.* Whenever his parents asked him about his plans, he concocted a new date to get his parents off his back. The fraudulent dates didn't help him or his parents. You need a real plan, but you also need to talk about its feasibility. A plan is useless if you don't revisit it now and then, and sidestepping the issue only serves to feed worry and increase aggravation levels.

Ian's two-week stay has turned into five years, and his mother's concerns have grown. "When I ask him about apartment hunting, he tells me rentals are too expensive and dismisses the topic. When he wasn't living at home, I was always glad to see him and wanted to know what he was up to. Now I want my storage closet back, which is behind his heaps of boxes and clothing. I look in his room—he's a guy who is clean and neat—and I say, 'How he can live in that hole?' I also worry about his social life. Maybe he has one and I just don't know about it."

Ian could ease his mother's feelings that he is taking advantage by including her more in his plans and by giving her a bit of insight into his social life—as much as he feels comfortable sharing. If she had more information, the mess he lives in might not bother her as much.

In her early twenties, Leila told her parents she would be home for one month. When the month became four, she and her parents went back to the drawing board. At that point Leila had a job and could help out financially, so she started paying a nominal monthly rent. The months turned into years—fifteen of them—during which no one brought up a good-bye date again. Everyone seemed content, but her mother silently wondered if living with her parents at age thirty-eight was the best idea for her daughter.

Avoiding the subject of a vacate date could be an excuse to ignore other troubles. Being ready to leave or to have a son or daughter move out could be a developmental as well as a marital issue, assuming an adult child or parent can afford to live elsewhere. You may believe enough is enough—your adult child should be on his own at this point—but your husband or wife campaigns for the status quo. Having another adult in the home can insulate a marriage: Husband and wife don't have to find things to talk about, as they can discuss their child's predicament and related topics.

When a plan seems stagnant or swerving in a wrong direction, it's time to communicate with each other. Marilyn's son is forty years old and has never been on his own. "I've been as patient as I can be. Every six months or so we tell him he needs to leave, but then we don't follow up," Marilyn explains. "We keep thinking the situation will change. We make attempts to talk, but he is adamant that he knows what he is doing and we shouldn't ask.

"We used to go out to dinner and the movies with our son, and now we're always arguing. This is not the relationship I wanted at this point in all of our lives. I feel my son has problems and should be seeing a therapist; my husband thinks I'm overreacting. I'm not in a good place and feel as if I did something wrong."

Without guidelines and goals, routines can get set in stone. In a matter of months, it feels as if it's too late, too embarrassing, or too difficult to bring up the subject. Yet it's vital to do so—for the big issues as well as the small ones. Who shops, who cleans, and who cooks don't appear to be deal breakers, but they can certainly create anxiety and tension. You think the details will work themselves out. You think your parent will do your laundry or have dinner on the table (she always did) . . . and some will. If you can't or don't want to continue your former role, it's critical to the new relationship that this be made clear.

For Elizabeth, admittedly not everyone, the responsibility of preparing meals was a huge issue, and she stated her position before her daughter moved in with her husband and granddaughter. She stated her feelings: She was finished with cooking. Diane listened, and does virtually all the cooking—no hard feelings.

No One Is a Mind Reader

You could be living together for months or years before something begins to annoy you. You thought you knew what life would be like because, like so many, you painted the scene in your head with broad strokes. What seems unimportant or insignificant goes unmentioned at the beginning, only to eventually become a constant source of irritation. You move in with Mom and Dad, stepparents, or in-laws with a glowing picture in your head, ignoring the nitty-gritty, such as what foods you eat (or don't), the hours you keep, who drives whom to work if several people share one or two cars, and so on.

Sophia is a case in point. She saw her mother and stepfather's home as a refuge after her divorce and surgery—a place to sort out what to do next and to get back on her feet. She didn't see beyond the fact that she would have a garage to store her furniture, massive amounts of wedding gifts, some still unused after two years of marriage, and a life's worth of memorabilia. Her mother didn't explain what she wanted Sophia to do or how she and her husband lived their lives, or what they expected from her. After a month of niceties that allowed

Sophia to recuperate from surgery, the things they hadn't discussed turned to unpleasantness.

"We have entirely different eating habits. When you're used to eating lightly and heavy meals with meat and potatoes are put in front of you every night, it's stressful, and made more so when they keep telling me I'm too picky," says Sophia. "Our sleep patterns don't coincide and became more out of sync after I got a job which required me to work long and late hours. My stepfather thinks my sleeping in is laziness, and both of them make noise around 6:30 a.m. to try to wake me up. My mother let me bring my dog, but then confined him to my room. It's just one thing after another with them."

You can't live up to expectations if you don't know what they are. Everything about living with her in-laws makes Nicole happy, except when her father-in-law gets huffy and silent and she can't decipher why.

You can't live up to expectations if you don't know what they are.

"All he has to say is, 'Please tie up the recycling and put the bottles out.' Or, 'We left a mess in the kitchen last night; would you mind . . .' Instead, he makes sarcastic, childish comments or drops stupid hints and pouts. I'm grateful to be able to live with them, and I'll do anything, but he has to tell me what he'd like; I don't want to guess."

At age fifty-five, Ann joined her mother in her childhood home. She and her mother weren't worried about getting along in the slightest. "Mom and I figured it would work fine. We'd save money. We'd share chores. I could gas up the car and she could clean. Oh sure, as a teen I couldn't get away from my mother fast enough, but none of those old issues seemed likely to cause trouble now. At eighty-three, Mom pretty much doesn't care how much makeup I put on, and I rarely date boys anymore with too much hair." Ann and her mother didn't discuss Ann's dating and where it might lead. It's a constant concern to Ann's mother, but she says nothing. Even at this point, three years into sharing the house, Ann's mother would worry less if they talked about the possibility of Ann being in a serious relationship. Asking about or communicating concerns and rules is the best way to solve the problem, or understand what's going on.

Minus a frank discussion, putting yourself in the other person's shoes sheds some light on how he or she feels, and on how you can help them become better able to react to disturbing events when they crop up. These examples analyze how the relatives you live with might feel so you can act accordingly . . . or try to.

You're fresh out of college and understand that having you in the house is an inconvenience for your parents. Your parents won't admit that. You're not a kid anymore who has to be told to clean up her room. You know what has to be done. You also know that if it were your home, you would want others to keep their things orderly and clean and to pitch in without being asked.

You're a single male in his late twenties or thirties, returning home, and you might like a woman to spend the night sometime. You rewind to your high school dating days. Your father stayed up until the young lady of the moment went home. You remember being torn: You wished he would go to bed and, at the same time, felt guilty for keeping him up. Unless your father has had a dramatic change in attitude, it's highly probable that he feels exactly the same way now. You could respect his feelings. You also could ask him if he has a different position now that you're an adult. It's worth a shot to ask.

You move into a community for fifty-fives and bring your mother-in-law along with you. You think this is a model situation; she'll meld into the community, join in the activities provided (bridge games and concerts are right up her alley), make new friends, and be happy. She doesn't, and you can't imagine why, since there are more people in her age bracket than yours.

Frequently, viewing the situation from someone else's perspective isn't enough, and that's because no one can read another person's mind. The mother-in-law in question received invitation after invitation to participate, but she ignored them. Why?

If you want answers or changes, you'll have to ask. If you want the sink wiped out after every use, you will have to alert everyone that this is how things are done in your home—or down the road there will be an explosion from pent-up resentment about something you never gave a thought to. If you want to initiate firmer rules about your young children's bedtimes or a reduction in the snacks Grandpa doles out too liberally, you'll have to speak up. If you want more help around the house or more money added to the household "pot," you will have to make your wishes known.

If you want answers or changes, you'll have to ask.

FAMILY MEETINGS RESOLVE ISSUES QUICKLY

The huge difference between now and when you lived as parent and child or sibling and sibling is that you can have a conversation, a dialogue of the sort you couldn't have back then. Then parents talked *at* their children, not with them. As adults, the conversation can be two-way.

Family meetings make it easier to address unanswered questions, and to bring up the "small stuff" that can lead to hysterics if left unresolved. Request a meeting whenever you are unhappy or see a potential problem. If family meetings become part of how your family functions once you've started them, they will be an incentive for everyone to think about what changes they want, to evaluate new needs as they arise, and to reconsider expectations that aren't being met.

Let it be known that anyone can call an impromptu or "emergency" family meeting. It can be as formal or informal as you'd like—around the dining room table, or in the den. Whatever the format, family meetings give everyone the chance to brush up on their communication skills and learn to relate more appropriately and sensitively to each other. Establish meeting rules that are fair to all parties and prevent free-for-alls and personal attacks.

Family Meeting Guidelines

- Put one person in charge and change the leader for each meeting.

- Give each person the chance to air their grievances (a one-minute time limit will keep the meeting focused).

- Ask who has a request or need if it is not apparent.

- Take notes if that is helpful, to ensure all issues are covered.

- Decide as a unit how to implement changes fairly.

- Remind everyone when you meet next—next week, next month.

- Meet at the scheduled time even if there are no "issues" to address; use the time to talk about what's going on in everyone's life.

LOWERING EXPECTATIONS

Family talks will resolve most problems, like who feeds the dog or waters the plants, or who cooks the meals or mows the lawn. While these are important issues, the overarching dilemmas that arise from our goals for our parents or children, or from their own dreams or missions, may have to be reduced to keep harmony and preserve the love you feel for each other.

Arminta Jacobson, the director of the Center for Parent Education at the University of North Texas, points out that parents with higher incomes "are usually more dissatisfied with their kids moving home . . . They expect their kids to get good jobs and make it on their own the way they have." Across the board, the economic strains being felt by most families are reason enough for parents to try a temporary lowering of expectations.

Granted, it's frustrating when it looks as if your offspring isn't trying to find a job or isn't working at retraining to prepare to get one. It's likewise upsetting when an in-law takes over the running of your household. And, it's hard to live with a parent's overt worry and constant badgering. Is it possible to change that parent or grown child? You can hope the answer is "yes," but, more likely, it will be difficult. Work around what you can't change, and instead, work to change how you think about the person or situation.

Work around what you can't change, and instead, work to change how you think about the person or situation.

"I had to recognize that my children are adults at this point," says David of his twenty-nine- and thirty-five-year-old sons, who have been living at home since they graduated from college. "I worry about how they will manage life on their own, but I've learned to accept them for who they are—not who I would like them to be, or thought they would be."

When hopes go awry, everyone will be happier with the living arrangements if you back off and lower your expectations. But, it's tricky to know when you have lowered your expectations too far and crossover into enabling. Joyce worries about her son's earning ability and makes excuses for him when she (and he) might feel better if she pushed him a bit more. "I raised a child who is too nice," she thinks. "He's not aggressive enough when it comes to earning money. I don't see any point in trying to change him. I think he was born sweet-natured and can't be anything but that."

It's fine to dream high for yourself and for those in your family, but upping the realism quotient will reduce everyone's feelings of disappointment and failure—and possibly salvage the relationship long-term. "My wife and I kept our expectations minimal because our daughter rejected our bourgeois attitudes and our values early on." George, seventy, refers to his youngest daughter, who got into drugs and led a fairly promiscuous life in her twenties. "She made our lives miserable for a few years because she had gone so far off the track. I wanted to throw her out, but didn't. My thinking was that some chronologically aged kids have not caught up emotionally; they need more time. She matured emotionally and socially very slowly, and, fortunately, I understood that. She turned the corner eventually, finished medical school, and she, her mother, and I are very close now."

Lowering expectations takes the pressure off everyone in the family. Salvaging the relationship as George and his wife did with your child or parent is more important than carping on what's not progressing as you had envisioned it would as long as you don't go too far and become an enabler.

KEYS TO LOWERING EXPECTATIONS

- Decide what's most important.
- Try to ignore what you're pretty sure you or your relative can't or won't change.
- Focus on the positive aspects of the relationship.
- Be accommodating whenever and wherever you can.
- Let each person devise his or her own destination . . . and accept it in a supportive manner.
- Strive for clarity in each person's role and adjust your expectations of individual contributions and responsibilities as circumstances change.
- Understand that if communication is poor and conversations are limited (or absent altogether), someone will be disappointed, unhappy, or resentful.

Chapter Four

Money Matters

WHAT WE MAY NEED AND EXPECT FROM FAMILY IS COMPOUNDED when the element of money is introduced. How money questions are approached and managed can be the glue that keeps family together or the delicate china plate that shatters it apart. Even though you may think money should not be part of the family equation, it is, and it's a big part. A plan, however sketchy, keeps this emotionally laden subject on the back burner so it's not a constant source of strife.

As everyone knows, you can be on top of the money tree one day, and then the branches get shaken and you fall rapidly to the bottom. The economy may have already forced your family to pool their resources, to depend solely on a parent's or an adult child's income or savings, to chip in when possible, or to provide assistance in lieu of funds.

Family members move in together for medical reasons, convenience, pure affection, or to assuage loneliness, but most moves are financially driven. The decision is a basic mathematical problem. You and your parents, for instance, own separate homes, but the upkeep and mortgage payments are more than one or both of you can afford. Your parent may be healthy, but a move to a senior community with its carrying charges and monthly fees may be out of reach for her (or your) limited income. In a different scenario, a 20 percent pay cut in the form of fewer days working or an across-the-board reduction in your

---

What Your Parent May Be Thinking

"I think we made a big mistake. We set a precedent of not taking money from our son, but we should have, and then stuck to it. Paying something would be the grown-up, mature thing to do. He has a job — granted, part-time — with some money coming in. I've told him that, but he has to come to it himself. If he gave us money, just a little bit, it might diffuse the feeling I have that he's intruding at the same time I appreciate his help."

Wendy's son, thirty-three, has been living at home for five years.

---

paycheck could make it impossible to meet your financial obligations. In this or similar financial jams, moving your children, partner, and you into your parents' home is a viable answer.

Living with a relative solves many financial problems, but, like expectations, you must straighten out the details in the beginning and adjust them along the way so everyone feels the

---

What Your Adult Child May Be Thinking

"I had over $100,000 in outstanding undergraduate and graduate school loans. I'd be paying them off for many years if my parents wanted rent. Living rent-free, I've been able to make a huge dent in what I owe. By allowing me to live with them, I will be a debt-free professional much sooner."

Lisa, at thirty, is finishing her third year as a corporate lawyer.

---

arrangement is fair. It may be that money isn't paid in by everyone, but as long as everyone agrees, not paying a portion of
expenses works. Misunderstandings and problems begin and
the warm feelings you have for each other get tarnished when
one person feels cheated or used.

In These Changing Times

You probably hadn't planned on living with your parents
again, or having your parents or another relative settle in with
you and your family. A trial run of a few weeks or a monthlong
visit would let you know if a long-term arrangement is feasible.
Generally, finances don't allow for this luxury; you or someone
in your family needs support quickly:

- Dad loses his job or has a pension too small to live on.

- A daughter just out of college can't find employment.

- You're older, fired, and have no other means of
  supporting yourself, your spouse, and your children.

- Credit card debt mounts, or you have enormous loans to
  repay.

- It doesn't make dollar sense to own or rent two places—
  two can live more cheaply than one.

- You can cover some of your bills, but not all of them.

A young adult child can spring his arrival on you. Deb-
ra's son, who is twenty-six, asked her to have dinner with him

and then explained that he and his roommate had real issues with their apartment. "We can't keep it," he told his mother. She asked the obvious, "Where are you going to go?" Home, naturally. He said he would be moving back home the following week, but he arrived the next day. His mother recalls, "It was very funny—that big serious dinner discussion—and fast."

The strain of meeting expenses for additional people has the potential to fracture once-model relationships. Scott's sixty-one-year-old mother had lived independently since her divorce from Scott's father when he was in high school. When she lost her job, Scott and his sisters paid their mother's rent, car insurance, and provided for whatever else she needed until it became too costly to keep her in her own place. She moved in with her son, who says their relationship—which he described as excellent when she lived on her own—has deteriorated to the point where he can barely talk to her.

The strain of meeting expenses for additional people has the potential to fracture once-model relationships.

Scott explains: "She relies on me for her financial well-being. I've already doled out over $50,000 to support her. I've explained that she can file for food stamps, but she refuses. I've suggested she expand her job search beyond the type of company she used to work for. She refuses. She says she's working on a plan, but won't share it. I'm coming out of a divorce and trying to rebuild my own life after depleting all my reserves to care for her. She's a grown woman who should respect the fact that you have to do things for the person who supports you, or at the very least, try to budget and listen to advice."

Scott's mother feels as if her son owes her; and in his opinion, his mother is behaving irrationally. They are at odds about most things financial, and that spills into their daily interactions. In circumstances like these, calling in a mediator or seeing a therapist or another impartial negotiator would help Scott and his mother learn to compromise, and, most importantly, communicate so they can work out their financial problems.

When money is tight, most families do what they have to even if it means being more watchful of their own spending. Rita's daughter called asking to come home with her husband, eighteen-month-old, and three-year-old, shortly after her son-in-law's business bellied up and left him with crushing debt. When Rita asked how long they could hold out, her daughter said they needed to move in the next weekend. They've been living with Rita and her husband for more than three years.

"It's more important that they get out of debt than they leave our house," says Rita. "They both work, the children go to day care, and I'm busier than ever with my full house . . . but I'm loving it."

The consensus: Family steps up to the financial plate in whatever ways they can. Like Rita, few resent helping their relatives if they can afford to. They don't mind the increase in grocery bills and the added wear and tear on the house unless they don't feel their support is appreciated or the person they are helping is not making an effort to fix his or her financial problems.

THE GENERATIONAL DIVIDE

Money has subtle layers beyond the hard cash to pay debts and expenses, current or future. Attitudes about spending and saving and what's equitable vary from family to family and person to person, depending on someone's age, financial stability, and earning power. No matter how financially secure, the majority of people watch where their money goes, and their perspective is strongly influenced by their individual background, successes and failures, and their generational leanings.

Expect differences of opinion because you and your parent are from different generations. Your views about money could be extremely contrary to those of your parent or offspring. You may have no qualms about giving anyone and everyone a status report on your bank account or stock portfolio, or you may hold your finances close to the chest. A parent who lived during the Great Depression is often reluctant to discuss financial matters or to ask for help. Dubbed the "Silent Generation" by *Time* magazine in the early 1950s, this group suffered great financial hardships as children and learned not to discuss the family's circumstances. Those raised by parents of the Silent Generation are likely to worry and be frugal, as are those with average fixed incomes. In contrast, higher-earning baby boomers and their children as a whole are more likely to spend—and talk about it.

Your views about money could be extremely contrary to those of your parent or offspring.

Dissimilar attitudes about money or how it's managed can set off disagreements or make your elders uncomfortable when the subject comes up. An eighty-five-year-old parent told me she thinks her daughters are wasteful; they spend too much on clothing, getting their nails done, and purchasing accessories, but true to her generation, she keeps those thoughts to herself. One of the daughters thinks her mother, who can afford new outfits, insists on wearing "old, ratty clothes." The spend-versus-save mentality will be the nucleus of arguments if you push your opinions on someone else.

Ann complains about a nonfunctioning burner on the stove in the house she shares with her mother. On mentioning that they should replace the thirty-year-old range, her mother, who is in her eighties, comes back with, "When do I use all four burners?" The old stove remains in place, and Ann, who does none of the cooking, decided to drop the subject. It's important to recognize and respect where your parent may be coming from and not force the issue of spending when it runs counter to what your parent believes.

Kimberly and her father disagree on how to tackle several money matters. "We have issues because my dad was raised in the Depression and was a youth during World War II," she clarifies. "When the economy tanked and he lost fifty percent in the down market, I wanted to fire his broker, but my dad wouldn't let me. He sits at his desk going over and over his statements. When I say, 'This is business . . . you have to handle it as business,' he ignores me. I remind him that we can't put our lives on hold because of the economy."

Kimberly grew up with the media consistently hyping change, but her father spent his formative years following Roosevelt's ideas—if you hung in there, everything would be okay. It was the prevalent attitude then, and it worked. We won the war and the economy turned around. Constancy was the byword during the World War II years, and it created a comfort level with people and things familiar. That, in part, explains her father's (and his peers') reluctance to get rid of his broker or change his financial ways.

Today's economic instability has affected more than what's in people's brokerage and bank accounts. For many, particularly newcomers to the workforce, the way we work and the ability to hold a full-time job has entered a new phase. Typically, when baby boomers finished school, they got jobs, found places to live, and supported themselves. Like other boomer parents, Joyce, sixty-four, refers to her twenty-six-year-old son as "underemployed," and she and her husband support him, excluding his gas, credit card, and cell-phone bills which he covers with income from part-time work.

When he first arrived home, Joyce had difficulty watching him languishing in the freelance world and in a field she didn't understand. "He's an online journalist, a job I interpret as having no security. It's taking me a long time to comprehend that this is the way his generation works. The work ethic is so different today."

The baby boomer attitude of "stand on your own two feet" is so much harder to achieve than it used to be. We all agree that it's more difficult to make it on your own as a young person today. It's just hard to reconcile the reality that grown children need support when parents worked hard, worked overtime, and took second jobs, and for the most part, it often seems like their children do not. To keep tensions minimal, boomer parents have to accept that how young adults view work—and working hard—is different from the way they did. Because the generations have different views on work and money, you will want to talk through how much should be spent or contributed, and by whom. The handling of money will be a constant source of conflict unless sorted out to everyone's satisfaction.

YOUR FAIR SHARE

If you are used to shopping for two or buying one potato and one apple as a single person, having more mouths to feed is an additional expense. When your financially strapped adult child joins you, it is generally not a question of who pays for what, but more an issue of whether your adult child should contribute. Hesitancy and doubt creep in when assisting adult children, even as reduced employment opportunities and changes in the way work is assigned complicate this already-difficult predicament for parents.

Parents who used to send checks to help subsidize their offspring's rents, to help them purchase places of their own, or to make ends meet so their adult children could live independently, now send different messages—"We're not paying your rent anymore," or "We can't send as much as we used to," or, more emphatically, "Come home; we're not supporting two households," particularly if it means dipping into funds reserved for retirement.

For a generation of children perpetually on the receiving end, this announcement that "the party is over" is a wake-up call to the fact that life will be different for most of them from now on. Mom and Dad were their backup, and parental support allowed them to live in the style they had grown accustomed to. The days of being a "trust fund" young adult, living off the income and benevolence of parents, are more limited than in recent history, as parents have watched their nest eggs and pensions shrink. Monies they counted on are less, and they worry about their own long-term financial security, whether or not they continue to work.

A *Money* magazine/ICR (International Communications Research) poll found that "60% of Americans believe college graduates should be allowed to move back home for up to a year, although 57% think the grads should be charged some rent." It's hard to charge rent if your children aren't working, but if they are, working out the details eliminates feelings of being used, or feelings of being the "user" who soaks up the kindness of others, his or her parents, in dollar bills.

"My son quit his full-time job knowing he had parent who would cushion him," says Suzanne. "He likes money; he grew up with it . . . I thought he would be driven by that. I keep a roof over his head and he earns enough freelancing to keep body and soul, but not enough for a nice apartment. He doesn't pay me anything; perhaps he should."

Speak directly to your adult child (or parent) if you have a problem with his or her money management. Out of college four years, Adam maxed out his credit card and found himself saddled with a $20,000 debt from being out of work and

Speak directly to your adult child (or parent) if you have a problem with his or her money management.

partying too much, by his own admission. His parents invited him to live with them. "We talked on the phone before I came home about what I had to do and what they expected in return. They knew I had no money, but they told me that I had to find a job quickly and start paying down my credit card without any help from them. In return for free room and board, I was to be their handyman on my days off. My parents outlined house projects they had lined up. My first priority was to find a job. They made their rules pretty clear without being angry at my frivolous spending and gross irresponsibility."

Larry's mother Elaine asks very little of her son and thirty-year-old daughter, who also lives with her. She's a single mom who has been supporting her two children by herself since Larry, twenty-seven, was three years old. Larry returned home when his roommates both lost their jobs, and paying the rent on his three-nights-a-week waiter's salary and tips was out of the question. As his mother tells it, "He says he wants to help and says he'll start paying me soon, but first he's saving. When I asked him what he was saving for, he told me he was saving for an HD-TV. He already has a twenty-seven-inch TV in his room. You know who bought that—not him. Right now I can afford to support him. When I think about insisting, I say to myself, 'Someday I may be destitute and on his doorstep.'"

Those who reject Elaine's approach as spoiling or not helping him take control of his life ask for some kind of monetary contribution from their adult children. Parents might try any of these options or a combination thereof with employed offspring.

Contribution Choices for Employed Offspring

- Select a reasonable token weekly or monthly "rent."

- Start an "Exit Fund" by taking xx dollars a month and putting it in a savings account to be given back at the end of the stay.

- Have your child agree to put a certain amount into savings on his own.

- Use the monthly "rent" to help run your house.

- Be precise about what an adult child is responsible for— his own clothing, car payments, credit card—and what parents will pay for: food and insurance, for example.

When you wrestle with the question of financial support for your adult children, consider that there is something to be said for providing it long-range. The Longitudinal Study of Generations has been examining relationships in families and how they change over time since its inception in 1971. The study found that by supporting children longer, they are more likely to help their parents financially—and emotionally—in parents' later years.

You may feel Elaine's son is taking advantage and fall more into the school of thought that having an adult child share in the expenses (even minimally) teaches them responsibility, and psychologically makes them proud, as it does with older parents who "pay in."

When Eileen and her husband were adding on to their home to make room for her in-laws, her in-laws offered money, and, as Eileen points out, "We didn't really need it, but we took it because we wanted them to feel as if it were their home, that they had a part in building it. We didn't want them to feel like guests."

POOLING RESOURCES

Sharing expenses improves a family's fiscal stability and that of the individuals in it. Pooling resources slashes costs and saves on everything from rent to electricity and food and home repairs. How you decide to manage expenses depends, of course, on individual circumstances and demands.

Kimberly and her father commingle their money and have a joint checking account. Her father deposits her paychecks and he is the family bookkeeper, but some of his excessive spending, quite counter to his other generational bent, gets to Kimberly. "For all his obsessing about the stock market, we do battle about how much money he spends on the dogs (we have ten dogs between us). He cooks them each a hamburger patty and hot dog every night for a snack. I calculated that the nightly indulgence plus their regular food costs us around $7,000 a year. He could shave off $3,000 to $4,000 a year if he cut out their lavish evening treat. We have the most obese dogs known to man, but they're loved.

"We argue some, but we're healthy communicators," Kimberly continues. "We say what we have to and we're fine five minutes later—although the regal treatment of the dogs remains unresolved."

Don't discount pride when your father offers his social security check. Your parent might insist on turning over his social security check to ease the financial burden of running the household, or to show gratitude for the living quarters you provide. A contribution allows for dignity and removes the demoralizing feeling of taking handouts at any age.

On the other hand, you may have a good reason for refusing a parent's check. Pamela, fifty-six, moved her mother in when running two households became too costly. She insisted her mother use her social security check for her own entertainment and personal needs since her mother had no other income stream. Pride didn't enter the picture for Pamela's mother; she happily spent the money on herself.

Stuck on the Giving or Receiving End

When a pattern has been set, it can seem as if you are stuck doling out the money or, conversely, being taken care of. The situation may feel lopsided. For the sake of argument, you relocate to live with and help your son and daughter-in-law financially so that they don't have to uproot their children. Be smart and ask how much they need, and about how long they anticipate they will need your monetary help. Determine a date—six months, a year from now—when you will reevaluate family finances together. Up-front discussions and even loose outlines help reduce the risk of ongoing money tension.

Up-front discussions and even loose outlines help reduce the risk of ongoing money tension.

You may have an adult child who does not appreciate your help and is not fiscally responsible. He or she, among other things, asks you to pay his credit card bill, spends money on things he can't afford, borrows from you often, and is slow to look for a job. To rectify this dilemma, depending on your son or daughter's long-range plans, state how long—a year, or eighteen months—you will provide a roof and basic support.

Show Your Appreciation

- Say "thank you" habitually for all things provided.

- Do what is asked in good time and in good humor.

- Anticipate the needs of others.

- Call on the way home to see if you should stop at the store to pick up groceries, or at the cleaners to pick up the clothes that are ready.

- Surprise the household by buying (or making) someone's favorite dessert, or giving a technology lesson if you're the family expert in such things.

- Offer to add more to your weekly or monthly contribution when you can, and *before* you are asked.

No paycheck? It's not the amount per se—it's the gesture. When the contribution can't be actual dollars and cents, providing services is a valid way to feel good about yourself, and it helps those you live with feel more positive about the arrangement because you are doing your part. By helping out, you balance the feelings of inequity that can arise. Young or old, people feel better if they contribute in some way:

grandparents caring for grandchildren, pulling the weeds or painting a porch for another family member who doesn't have the time.

Call it the barter system. Take or make your contribution out in trade: Do the laundry or yard work, baby- or pet-sit, do the shopping . . . Twenty-five-year-old Amanda's parents don't ask her to cook, but it's something she likes to do and does with a gourmet flair. On the rare occasions she has free time, she prepares special meals and leaves them in the refrigerator for her parents to find. She's not looking for a pat on the back or acknowledgment. It's her way of telling her parents she recognizes that she is privileged to be living rent-free and able to save for the home she hopes to buy one day.

Showing appreciation is often more than enough. "I had no concerns when my son and daughter-in-law came to live with us after my son lost his job," seventy-six-year-old Margery says. "My daughter-in-law never took advantage. She took care of her children, cleaned the house, and cooked. I worked and loved coming back to a home-cooked dinner every night. I hated the idea that they would leave at some point, but knew it was inevitable.

Showing appreciation is often more than enough.

"After my son had a job again and they had saved, they found a home they loved. They were short about $4,000, which my husband and I offered. They were going to pass up their dream house because they didn't want to take our money. It took some arm bending, but they finally did."

IT'S NOT ALWAYS ABOUT MONEY

The impetus for living together isn't always about failed businesses, debt, high rents, and job or home loss. For some it's a short-term medical setback and recuperation period, or wanting emotional support and company. When you call and your older parent says, "Yours was the only voice I heard today," you begin to feel that maybe your parent needs you even if he is financially solvent. Divorcees and widows of any age find that they, too, welcome the company of an adult child. They don't like coming home to an empty house, or decide they don't like living alone.

One widow in her sixties, who says she feels as if she's fifty, explained it this way: "When my son went to college and I started dating, I liked my privacy, but then I stopped dating and was happy to have him home."

Spry and healthy at eighty-six, Dorothy invited her daughter and granddaughter to live with her after Dorothy's husband died. Dorothy finds it rewarding to support her daughter and granddaughter. "Living together is ongoing in our family. At age nineteen I went from my family to my husband, and then my mother-in-law's home, and had never lived alone. I was really lonely when my husband died. Having my daughter live with me seemed like the thing to do. I took her from a nice-paying job to keep me company, so I feel like I owe her. I gave her a credit card and buy her whatever she and my granddaughter need. It's only fair."

Money questions can either be a constant thorn or a nonissue in the relationship, depending on the family's financial circumstances and, more importantly, the agreements you work out. Whether your new housemates are your son and his children, your in-laws, a wealthy parent, a jobless sibling, or your penniless college graduate, once you've made a plan, drop the money discussions.

PUTTING MONEY MATTERS IN THEIR PROPER PLACE

- Talk through money difficulties early on and reach reasonable agreements so that dollars-and-cents conversations can fade into the background.

- Keep money issues in the family. Don't discuss your family's financial agreements with your boyfriend or book club.

- Don't allow money to define or dominate the relationship.

- Separate money problems from other problems you may have with your relatives.

CHAPTER FIVE

PUSHING YOUR BUTTONS

A JOB LOSS, THE DISSOLUTION OF A MARRIAGE OR LONG-TERM relationship, the death of a parent or spouse, and changing residences are acute life stressors. The anxiety you may feel over finances adds another layer of discontent and worry. A move back in with relatives is usually accompanied by one of these significant stressors. The thorny circumstances that brought you together again were—and most likely will continue to be— disturbing for a while. And now, the people who are simultaneously your biggest fans and harshest critics are in close range. The only separation is the flight of stairs between upstairs and down, or the walls between a room or two.

When you lived on your own, the actual physical distance, whether a mile or a hundred miles, cushioned you against prickly annoyances. You could hang up the phone or leave for your own place if you didn't like what you were hearing or the way someone was acting. You're far more vulnerable now because of the conditions under which you decided to "room" together, and the easy access.

Before you were a unit under the same roof as grown-ups, you were better able to shrug off insinuations and needling remarks because they didn't affect your day-to-day life as recurrently or as intensely. When you're on edge or feeling uncertain about what's next in your life, irritants that might otherwise be ignored can trigger powerful flashbacks to periods from your childhood that, as an adult child or parent, you would rather forget.

Owning the house, paying the bills, or being older doesn't give you license to insult, control, or rebuke the people you live with. And being the child doesn't mean you can act like one, no matter what your age. You shouldn't expect your meals prepared without your helping, or to have neatly folded clean clothes at hand without having gone near the laundry room or a Laundromat.

Virtually everyone—young and old—has hot-button issues that become magnified when affronts or comments about them come from a parent, child, or sibling who knows you so well. Touchy subjects and irksome attitudes, although different from one person to the next, release a torrent of negative emotions and reactions. New living arrangements will be unpleasant if you and yours tread in these delicate areas. It can feel as if you were never independent. Or worse—you can feel unloved and underappreciated. When you pay attention to and steer clear of potentially explosive matters—yours and theirs—you eliminate unnecessary chafing, the kind that drives you and those you love crazy.

Age and accomplishments don't give you immunity against insults and personal attacks, or the anger they create.

Age and accomplishments don't give you immunity against insults and personal attacks, or the anger they create. Irving, an accomplished, seventy-year-old dentist, was ordered around by his controlling ninety-two-year-old mother. He tried to ignore her persistence, but her directives stung. "Can you believe she's telling me what to do?" he says with a self-deprecating tone. "I do what she asks even though the whole idea of her as Queen Bee still reigning makes me furious."

One might wonder why Irving didn't ask her to stop, but he was raised in a different time, one in which children, whatever their age, didn't question a parent's authority—even when it was excessive or power-driven. Rose Kennedy was known for instructing and criticizing her nine children. In 1964, her son, Ted, had just completed his first term as a U.S. senator. Following a plane crash, he spent months hospitalized in a Stryker frame, a contraption which renders a person immovable except to be occasionally turned over—faceup, staring at the ceiling, or facedown, staring at the floor. Rose sent Ted Kennedy frequent letters telling him to work on his writing and speaking. "When you are lying in bed, you can read a paragraph and then try to rewrite it or resay it." As *The Boston Globe* writing team notes in their book, *Last Lion: The Fall and Rise of Ted Kennedy,* she added, "Then notice the difference between succinct, dramatic impressions of the author and your (verbose) discursive, dull recital of the same events."

What Your Parent May Be Thinking:

"My daughter doesn't have her life together. She's almost forty and she has no money in the bank, huge debts, and little direction. It worries and angers me, so I keep after her the same way I did when she was an adolescent."

Nancy, sixty-four, has both of her adult children (ages thirty-four and thirty-nine) living with her.

What Your Adult Child May Be Thinking:

"My mom is fifty and so skinny; I'm heavier, but not overweight at all. My mother tells me to lose ten pounds if I want to wear that bathing suit or that dress. I'm not a child; I don't need to be told what to eat or how much I should weigh. She needs to stop implying that I am fat and trying to remold me."

Heather, twenty-four, has been living at home since she graduated from college.

The Parent-Child Trap

You are likely to view the relationship differently now. Life experiences have given you a different perspective, a different tolerance level and different needs. When Nancy's then-thirty-four-year-old daughter returned home five years ago, Nancy was so unhappy she took over her daughter's life, telling her what to do next in terms of going back to school. As Nancy tells it, there were a lot of angry words on both sides. Pitting a mother's desires against an adult child's lack of motivation is a design for ill-tempered coexistence. Nancy's daughter butted heads with her mother and refused to become the obedient child again.

Heather, on the other hand, "gets" her mother and allows herself to become the child to her mother's parent—mother belittling, daughter not liking it, but taking what her mother disgorges. They assume their long-ago roles. Not everyone, Nancy's older daughter included, wants to or can comply with someone else's demands or insults. They sound alarms for those wanting to escape, or thought that they already had, the parent-child trap.

This common trap is a throwback to how you functioned as parent and child, not as you are now, adult and adult. It's so easy to get stuck in the parent-child trap again because it works both ways: The parent continues to parent and the adult child continues to act like his or her ten-year-old self, slipping back into allowing Mom or Dad to take over, doing again what they did for you when you were a child.

Be watchful to avoid being caught in residual parent-child entanglements: you acquiescing to your parent's mandates, or you as the parent spouting criticism like a sergeant in the Fourth Regiment, dressing down soldiers with unpolished boots. Your new role, be you the parent or the adult child, is to spot and curb Mom/Dad/child ways of relating without resorting to harsh accusations as self-defense mechanisms.

Be watchful to avoid being caught in residual parent-child entanglements.

As a child, circumstances may have forced you into a parenting role. A divorce instilled an overblown sense of obligation to watch over and protect your mother or father. Or, you may have had an incompetent or alcoholic parent, and had to step in to ensure that your younger siblings had done their homework and packed their school lunches. You took charge and made sure the household ran well. As an adult child, continuing to watch over, cover for, or bail out your parent is essentially the parent-child trap in reverse.

Babying the "Baby"

One of the most blatant parent-child entrapments is the parent who continues to treat you like a baby or preteen, or the adult child who continues to be his parent's parent. That parent makes sure you have money when you go out; she reminds you to wear a jacket or take an umbrella, to comb your hair, floss your teeth, or pack your cell-phone charger. The tendency to think of you as irresponsible (as you may well have been as a kid), making sure you do what you are supposed to, comes from years of protecting you and ensuring your safety. But, look carefully before you place blame. Often these adult children are guilty of enjoying being taken care of, and happily allow a parent to be the architect of their comings and goings, and to provide their survival basics without pitching in.

Since babying the baby can operate the other way too, adult children may want to rethink how they interpret not only how they are being treated, but also how they might be reverting to their childlike status again. You may have been "Daddy's little girl" growing up. Are you still? Your father's and your view about whom you date could be miles apart. Even as an adult, his warnings and comments upset and influence you. On all issues, but particularly on those involving your social life, assess whether your parent's concern is real or simply another form of regarding you as a youngster and expecting you to concur.

Consider that parents' reactions to you may have validity. Perhaps you have a history of dating inappropriate people, of being careless with money, or of not focusing on the task at hand—and you still do. Your parents guided you for decades;

truth be told, they've had to rescue you many times, and that could justify how they act now. If, on the other hand, you've actually taken responsibility in an area where you previously didn't, explain the "changed you" and how you would like to be treated now.

Whatever your former dependency or current "reform," your parent is no longer tying your shoelaces or signing your permission slips. You cut the apron strings long ago, or should have. Watching over you is an ingrained habit, often unnoticed by parents themselves, and therefore, impossible for them to stop without your not-so-subtle guidance. You can modify a parent's behavior by being respectful and avoiding hurtful words. Similarly, if you are a parent who no longer wants your adult child behaving like your parent, reassure her that you are capable and can be in charge of yourself.

You Might Say:

- "It's true, I didn't take care of things when I was younger, but I'm very responsible now."

- "I appreciate your concern, but I can handle it myself."

- "Thank you for offering to make the call for me, but I'll do it."

- "I know your intentions are good, but it offends me when you continue to . . ."

- "I really want to choose my own gift for my friend's wedding. I have something specific in mind."

Escaping the Parent-Child Trap

As the parent or adult child, you'll want to examine if and how you perpetuate the parent-child trap. Siena, the mother of an unemployed thirty-two-year-old attorney, admits she can't help herself when her daughter prepares for a job interview. "I'm thrilled at the prospect of a job for her and say, 'Let's pick out your clothes.' If she's already picked which suit she's wearing and I'm opposed, I tell her I don't think that outfit is her most becoming or the best selection. I know I shouldn't interfere, but I want her to look good, and I know what looks best on her."

A fine line exists between the parent (like Siena) who makes decisions that you're perfectly capable of making yourself, and the doting parent whose nature is to nurture—that's just how that parent is: a mom who can't resist buying her adult child another book, or baking her favorite dessert, or a dad who hands you two tickets to a baseball game. Before you blurt out "That's another thing I didn't ask for (or don't need)," decide which parent type you are dealing with—one who is naturally over-nurturing, knows what you like, and is genuinely pleased to provide it whenever he or she can, or one who wishes she still had young children to coddle?

Adult children are not beyond coddling and hovering over their parents—even high-functioning ones. You've had a lot of life experiences, including starting and making a success of your own business. You don't like the way your mother handles problems where she works. Your stance is that she should stop allowing her coworkers to boss her around; you

Adult children are not beyond coddling and hovering over their parents.

bring up the subject persistently. She has asked you to let it go, but you keep at her, even when she tells you she's had her job for twenty years and is quite satisfied with how things are.

Paula, a single mother of two grown sons, has lived with her seventy-two-year-old father for the past two years, and worries about his driving. She transferred her fear for her sons' safety on the road to her dad, and he doesn't like it. "Whenever I get in the car, my daughter shouts, 'Drive carefully.' I feel as if I just got my license, even though I've been driving for over fifty years and have a perfect record—no speeding tickets, no accidents. It's kind of insulting. I'm the one who's supposed to be protecting her," says Paula's father.

As an adult child or parent, look back and ask yourself if there is a pattern that needs breaking. Are you perpetuating a cycle of babying that your parent started? Or, one you started with your parent years ago?

"My daughter doesn't think I can do anything right," Anita, seventy, complains. "She tells me what to wear and how to sell to customers in my flower shop. She has something to say about everything I do, from how I wash the floor to how I fold T-shirts. This handling me as if I'm hopeless started when she was a teenager; she feels as if she's saving me. From what? I have no idea."

Paula's father reminds his daughter of his driving record and asks her to stop, and Anita feels she's making headway with her daughter the only way she can—by ignoring the advice her daughter hurls at her. Announcing when you don't like something or how you feel is often sufficient for a parent or adult child to change the propensity to protect, shield, or baby, but the realization may not take hold the first time you mention it.

It's always more effective to send "I" messages—"I pay for my clothes"; "I feel this way"; "I'm troubled"; and so forth—because the "I" message is usually devoid of blame or advice. But, sometimes a "You" message is a strategy that works in spite of the fact that you-messages finger-point and label. For example, each time you are asked (or reprimanded) to put your laundry away, to drive safely, or use more soap on the dishes, add amusement or kindness in your voice to soften the judgments you're making. Keep in mind that with your parent or adult child, you have to be more respectful than you'd be with the parent or adult child with whom sarcasm or humor is acceptable. The fluidity of your relationship affects your response.

You Might Say: "There you go again, treating me as if I'm five years old." (Or fifteen, or whatever age you feel you would be regressing to if you say nothing.)

If your parent has a witty sense of humor, you could say: "You're being silly again. I lived on my own for twenty years; it's amazing I didn't die of malnutrition."

If your relationship is close and strong, be bold and say: "Please stop (asking me, telling me, making up my mind for me)."

Olivia isn't the neatest of thirty-year-olds, and her father still gets angry with her for having a cluttered room. He wants an unobstructed path from the door of her room to the window on the other side. Olivia has a standard comeback which she gives with a smile: "I say, 'Dad, you're not buying my clothes anymore. Since I pay, I have the right to toss my things anywhere I like.' He agrees, but just keeps riding me about how messy I am, even though I give him the same response every time he mentions the condition of my room."

Parents of adult children don't necessarily see this and other similar situations as babying. What they see is a messy house, an ignoring of their advice, or a continuation of the parenting role they were sure they were long done with. It's frustrating for parents to cajole regularly, and becomes tiresome, especially when they have other things to occupy their thoughts and time.

Parents can avoid parent-child traps by, in Olivia's case, avoiding her bedroom entirely. Parents can also let go of the unimportant things and concede that their adult child will do things his or her way, regardless of how displeased a parent gets. Think about what you could do with all the energy you would save by ignoring what bothers you and converting it in your head and actions to what *used to* bother you. In that way, whatever it is becomes a button that can no longer be pushed.

If repetitive prompts don't cure the habit, you can try to view the impasse this way: Tell yourself that babying the grown-up you is a sign that your parent or adult child loves you.

Coping with Control and Manipulation

Loving you and running your life are not mutually exclusive. With cell phones, texting, and e-mail, parents who want to mastermind their adult children's lives or adult children who want to keep tabs on the their parents can do so without much difficulty. If you grew up in constant contact with each other, having another person know where you are every moment may not

Loving you and running your life are not mutually exclusive.

feel intrusive. You are so used to it that you don't see repetitive calls as a control issue.

An "out of sight, out of mind" attitude takes hold for many when son, daughter, or parent is not in the same home. Paula stopped worrying about her sons' driving when they stopped living with her, but returning home puts you on the "firing line." When her rent doubled, Stephanie, thirty-one, returned to live with her mother four years ago after being on her own since the age of eighteen. She noted her mother's immediate switch back to her old controlling ways. "I could have been lying in a gutter; she never called to check on me. Now that I'm home, I get phone calls all day at work asking where I am, when will I be home, and when I arrive, where have I been?"

Living together means that family members know your schedule: what time you get up, what you eat, what you wear, when you go out. Anticipate some difficulties. A clever, manipulative parent might camouflage efforts to control by saying one thing when you know he or she means another. "Do whatever works for you. Don't worry about me." What she probably means is worry about me and do what I want. Then again, you could spot the blueprint immediately from your earlier years together. As Stephanie says, "After coming and going as I pleased, I knew life with my mother was going to be very problematic."

The manipulative adult child employs similar tactics. He or she will put a slight whine in the voice, turn a small need into an emergency, or use the same "Don't worry about me" line. Parents who are conditioned to please their children will fall for it—they'll change meetings or social engagements to be home, or drop everything to do what their child asks. Adult children know how parents have acted in the past and expect them to continue being "suckers" to their manipulations.

When you share the same house, running someone else's life or having yours maneuvered by others can make existence near impossible. If your son or daughter is married, some former parental control is lost by attrition to the spouse, but that doesn't prevent a goodly number of parents from maintaining as much control as possible. They give their opinions and make suggestions in ways that influence their offspring to strongly consider their input. It can become an unending battle between parent, adult child, and the adult child's partner.

For parents, the very real danger of vying for full control over a married son or daughter is loss of access to that grown offspring. A son- or daughter-in-law is gatekeeper by marriage to your child—and grandchildren. "My son-in-law is jealous of any time my daughter spends with me," explains Carmen. "He thinks I control her, but I know he's the one with all the power." This is a fruitless tug-of-war, and one Carmen needs to abandon, or she will have less and less time with her daughter even though they live in the same house.

Believing they know what is best and right for their child justifies many parents' attempts to control their adult offspring, and vice versa. Continuing to control an adult child is a recipe for disaster. You can't pull the strings anymore. Control issues can be far-reaching—from what time dinner is served and when you pay the bills, to how you dress your children or yourself— including going so far as to try to tell you with whom you should or shouldn't be friends. Your immediate reaction to the latter may be to go on the defensive: "Don't tell me who I should spend my time with," or, "Where I go is my business" (which is true), but such retorts only serve to raise everyone's ire. A less-provoking response is, "I know you're not fond of my friends, but I rather enjoy them." You might also agree with a valid objection by saying, "It's true, my friend Kirk parties too much, but underneath that playboy exterior, he's a pretty serious guy."

Believing they know what is best and right for their child justifies many parents' attempts to control their adult offspring, and vice versa.

In the case of friends who come in and out of the house, it may be that your parent worries about the image they reflect on the family. Your father sees himself as someone better or smarter, and wants you to have friends who underscore what he believes is the family's superiority or elevated social position—probably not unlike the way he reacted to your friends when you were a teenager. Or, a parent could denigrate your friends just so you give them up to spend more time at home.

When Scott, thirty-five, explains he will be away for the weekend, his mother can be counted on to say, "I thought you would be home. I was planning to make your favorite dinner." His mother's intention is to elicit guilt and make Scott feel as if he should cancel his plans, and, in this particular scenario, not leave his mother home alone for two days.

To intensify the guilt trip, his formerly independent, able, sixty-one-year-old mother who is living in his home, adds, "I took care of you; now it's your turn to care for me." Scott's not buying it. When a parent tries to manipulate, run through this quick checklist before you respond.

Evaluating Someone's Motivation:

- Is she well-intentioned?

- Is she overreacting?

- Am I overreacting?

- Am I being too sensitive?

- Am I being fair?

At times, the best reaction is no reaction, but rather a simple acknowledgment that you hear what is being said or advised. With a control freak in your midst, you may need to distance yourself by being away from the house more. When you honor your own wishes, the other person is less able to dictate your course.

You Might Say:
- "Wish I could stay home, but I can't. I promised to be there."

- "I'm happy you want to be with me. I'll be back before you know it."

- "No, I can't do what you're asking," said calmly. As an adult, it is your right to refuse any request that feels manipulative.

In reverse, parental guilt is a powerful control weapon that puts the adult child in charge and able to get what he wants from his parent. An adult child may use the past to manipulate his parents by making pointed references to the plays and recitals or sporting events they didn't attend, or the birthday parties, encouragement, or support not given.

Richard, sixty-six, was a superlative father who raised three children. He helped with homework, missed no performances, kept the family cars in working order, and made delicious, complicated dinners most nights. His twenty-nine-year-old daughter moved home, and she pushes Richard's guilt button just by being there; he can't shed his conscientious parent role. He and his wife rethink plans when their daughter raises her eyebrows and says, "Oh, you won't be home Saturday night—what will I do?" He swims in guilt if his daughter doesn't have a date or friends to see, and she knows looking glum will keep her parents home.

Even without direct references to the past from a grown child, the guilty parent feels an obligation to make up for omissions by doing whatever his or her adult child requests. "I was a lousy parent and made lots of mistakes," explains Donald, a retired factory foreman who lives with one of his sons, daughter-in-law, and two grandchildren. "I worked long hours and did very little with my children. My wife was in charge of the kids. I have great remorse for my failings as a parent, and am trying to make amends by helping with my grandchildren even when I really don't feel like it. I haven't missed one of grandson's swim meets. I feel great when my son says, 'Thanks for covering for me, Dad.' "

Put-upon parents are often so used to being taken advantage of that they have a hard time recognizing what's happening; this is because they are putty in the hands of their adult children. Mom may be exhausted from a tough week at work, but when her manipulative adult son asks her to go to the post office or drugstore for him when she's out running her own errands on Saturday, she capitulates. It's easy to coax an unsuspecting parent into doing your chores or including your friends for dinner with a little flattery. The dinner scenario goes something like this:

Adult son to Mom: "You're making lasagna? How about I invite Billy and Jess to join us? You make the best lasagna, and they love it as much as I do." This is said casually, as if it were a *fait accompli.*

This mother rarely said no to her offspring the entire time they were growing up. Although having a couple more people is no big deal, Mom hesitates, thinking, "I planned the leftovers for another night, and there won't be any if I feed Billy and Jess."

You Might Say
- "I'm flattered that you and your friends enjoy my cooking, but tonight is not a good night for company."

- Or, "Let's plan to have them come over one night when you're cooking."

- Or, "Lasagna is easy. I'll walk you through the recipe, and you can cook for your friends. Dad and I will join you."

- Or, "If your friends have dinner with us, you won't have any dinner on Monday. I won't be home that night, and thought you could heat up the leftovers. You'll have to make dinner for your father, too."

By turning the tables on your manipulative adult child, you let him know that you are not his (or his friends') private chef or gofer. By recognizing that your adult child is capable, parents can break the cycle of feeling put-upon and being on call for whatever con or manipulation their adult child springs on them.

SHORT-CIRCUITING CRITICISM

You may have seriously tried to turn in your "parent papers," but as anyone who is a parent knows, that is not entirely possible. With an adult child in your home, or you in theirs, ask yourself: Will I be able to hold my tongue when I don't agree with a decision I think impractical or a waste of time? Can I refrain from offering my opinion, which will surely be interpreted as criticism? Adult children who live with their highly critical parents again wonder how they will survive having their self-esteem chipped away at on a full-time basis.

Likewise, you may be an adult child who is critical of how your parent spends his money (or doesn't), how he exercises (or doesn't), or what books he reads (or doesn't). You may see no advantage or positive attributes to some of your parents' friends, and question why they spend time with them. You don't hesitate to tell your parents how boring or dull you think their friends are. You critique their friends for having nothing to add to a conversation, or for being too flashy or too brash— possibly in an effort to make your parents rethink with whom they socialize. All of this amounts to meaningless criticism veiled as opinion.

There is plenty of room for criticism on both sides when you live with each other. It's just as easy to take the positive approach—to praise or say nothing, and turn yourself into a parent or child's fan, especially when he or she is going through a rough period.

Sensitivity levels run high for a parent or adult child who has been unemployed for lengthy periods, or who may need to retrain or explore alternate avenues. You might inadvertently press that hot button without meaning to. Wanting to be helpful, you ask to look over an outgoing résumé, but to the job hunter, your inquiry might be seen as second-guessing or interfering. The job seeker interprets the offer as criticism: "You think I make careless mistakes," or "You don't trust me." Difficult as it may be, you are better off waiting until you are asked to assist. For those who resist help, the mere hint of what more they could be doing only underscores their feelings of inadequacy. Engaging in job-related discussions under such circumstances could erode the good relationship you once had.

Elaine's thirty-year-old daughter Alexia was a chubby child and has emotional scars from her teasing classmates. Her mother—who was under the impression food was a nonissue, since Alexia had slimmed down to a size six in high school and had stayed trim—stepped into perennial no-win territory. "I thought I was making an innocent comment when I said how good I thought the spare ribs were, and asked if she enjoyed them as much as I did. Oh, dear, what a mistake. She visibly bristled and let me have it about still watching what she eats."

If your adult child or parent has weight problems or had in the past, one glance in her direction while she's eating can ignite old battles you and she may have had over food in the past. She may be rail-thin now, but in her mind, she remains that blubbery person (kid or grownup), and your watchful eye or innocuous words will be construed as censure. Find something else to discuss. Richard, whose twenty-nine-year-old daughter fights her weight to this day wisely concludes, "My daughter weighs much more than she should and she doesn't exercise, but I've learned the hard way that a parent can wound an adult child so easily. It's a subject I don't ever mention anymore."

You're Wearing That?!

With all adults in the house, except for the grandchildren, you are probably aware that diet and exercise, politics, or employment, your mother or your daughter's revealing way of dressing, or a parent's gray hair you think should be dyed blond are personal choices, and probably off-limits. Yet, parent or child may continue to assess most things about the other's appearance, career, or parenting style and voice dissatisfaction—at least, it feels that way to the recipient. Direct, deliberate critiques are painful, and at times it may feel as if there's no end to the disapproval spewed at you. When you find yourself spending an inordinate amount of time trying to meet a parent's or offspring's high standards, it's time to reflect on how much of your efforts are designed to either thwart criticism or to gain approval.

In things fashion- and appearance-related, for instance, it tends to be the mother second-guessing a daughter's selection. Mom will say something like, "I thought you would wear the black top to Aunt Ingrid's party." The message her susceptible adult daughter hears is: "Mom thinks I look thinner, younger, more attractive, in black." The question you need to ask yourself is: Do you dress to please your parent, or yourself?

Daughters criticize their parents, too. Millie's forty-eight-year-old daughter mocks her mother's shoes without openly calling them old-lady shoes. "She checks me out every morning and says, 'Mother, really. Those are from the year one; you need to get rid of them. You're not going anywhere in those shoes, are you? What about the pair we bought last week, or the cute black pair with a little heel?' Why her obsession with what I put on my feet? I don't know. After two years in the same house, you'd think she'd leave it alone," says Millie. "When she didn't, I turned the shoe fiasco into good-natured ribbing. Every morning before she can say a word about my shoes, I say, 'You can't go out looking like that.' Now we race to see which one of us can make the first remark and end up laughing."

Everyone agrees that some criticism is constructive, but how you offer it will determine how well it's received—as helpful, or judgmental. Kimberly is tactless in her criticism of her seventy-nine-year-old father. Instead of offering to help him sort through his papers or to find a less-conspicuous place than the living room to keep them, she lashes out quite unproductively. Kimberly's dad gives his account. "She tells me I have a clutter problem and need to see a therapist. I'm an admitted pack rat, and have financial papers dating back fifteen years or more; the IRS might want to see them someday. Kimberly tells me to throw them out, but what if the tax man wants them? We argue about this a lot. I'm not going to change, and I'm not seeing a therapist."

With a hypercritical parent (or son or daughter), you may need to take an aggressive approach to stop the intensely bothersome innuendos and direct comments. It's nearly impossible to stave off the cutting edge of criticism without letting the person know how you feel.

You Might Say:

- "When you say that, I feel as if you are always judging me."

- "You know when you say things like that, you hurt my feelings. I'm sure you're not aware that you're doing it."

- "Your comment makes me feel as if I can't do anything right."

- "When you disapprove, I feel as if I don't measure up."

- "I feel like a failure with those constant remarks."

- "I know you mean well, but please stop (insert specific criticism)."

- "I already feel badly about (my job loss, my weight, my child's behavior or school performance); I don't need to be reminded."

- "When you criticize me, I will walk away every time" (and then do so until the old patterns are broken).

Moving Beyond Hot-Button Issues

Because you live together now, there are so many more opportunities to say and do things that are better left alone. Every time you criticize or try to control, you set the stage for argument and retaliation. While some parents and adult children will passively accept what's being said, others will come back with, "But, you always . . ." And so the war that cannot be won begins (or continues).

To avoid initiating or escalating disagreements, use the suggestions in the sidebar below to help improve communication. That's the most effective way to stop or curtail the irritations that keep you interacting in useless ways. Getting caught up in negative behaviors threatens to damage the relationship, along with your own feelings of well-being. When you enter sensitive terrain or rehash past transgressions, it doesn't matter if you are on the dishing-out or the receiving end: You may find yourself ending conversations with hurt feelings, or walking away saddled with guilt.

Not pushing each other's buttons creates an environment of respect and understanding, as well as validates that both of you are good people. By putting an end to the babying, controlling, and criticism, you are much more likely to move your relative from being a harsh critic to an ardent supporter.

ELIMINATING HOT-BUTTON ISSUES

- Review the history of the real or perceived "failing," because it may be outdated and irrelevant.
- Think before you blurt out something you know the other person is sensitive about.
- Evaluate how what you say may affect the other person.
- Count the number of times you criticize, manipulate, or instruct, and try to reduce that number.
- Make light of those behaviors that get to you by turning them into a joke you share.
- Act like the grown-up you are.

Chapter Six

From Bedroom to Den
and Back Again

Living room—what living room? It's now a playroom chock-full of children's brightly colored building blocks, a toy kitchen set, and piles of soft, cuddly stuffed animals. Your daughter's bedroom? You waited years to transform it into a gorgeous office, and you outfitted it just so. It's now your daughter's bedroom again, with a fabulous workspace, and you're back to taking care of business at the kitchen table. The sacrifice of sharing space, if you see it that way, won't loom so large once you have time to weigh the pluses against the minuses.

You may feel a bit overwhelmed at the idea of reassigning or finding space for your family member, but the logistics are less problematic than many financial or interpersonal issues you may be facing. The physical living space, while important, can be managed. Even those short on space aren't overly concerned. They turn the laundry room into an office or a married sister's bedroom into a baby's room. It's more important to be together and try to improve a parent or adult child's circumstances than to worry about a son and daughter-in-law living in the basement, or having to open the living-room couch each evening to make up a bed. Of the latter, Ruth, whose daughter, her husband, and three children moved in, says, "They took over the whole house. It's tight with the baby in a crib and a pullout sofa in the living room, but we're comfortable."

If there's room in your heart, there's room in your home for sons and daughters, parents, and in-laws who need a place to live. Yes, sometimes it may be cramped (or annoying) to have two people sharing the kitchen, toddlers underfoot, or a sloppy person leaving her possessions everywhere. Expect noise levels to escalate and space to seem smaller. When others move into your house or you into theirs, you give up the freedom to run around scantily dressed, and the option to use previously unoccupied rooms the way you used to. You also gain much more than you lose, as do those who join or rejoin the family.

Margery looks back: "We weren't home the week my son and his wife and children moved in. The wall behind one of the doors has a hole—something banged into it. I have never fixed it. Probably won't because it's a memento of the two fabulous years we had with them—years that gave my husband and me an indelible bond to our son, daughter-in-law, and grandchildren."

With no space for her toddler grandchildren to play, Rita, sixty-six, converted her dining room into a playroom. "It was originally a den for my children. I look at this change as a throwback to another happy time in our lives."

Ideally, everyone would have a separate entrance out of earshot to come and go as they please. It would be nice if no one bumped into each other in the kitchen or had to share a bedroom. Although the living arrangements are rarely optimum (very few homes have two kitchens), the majority of twenty-somethings believe that living with family solves many of their problems and gives them free or cut-rate housing *and* good meals. Even if it isn't a first choice, it's the best choice for right

> ## What Your Parent May Be Thinking
>
> *"When my daughter got divorced, we squeezed. She and her two young children shared my spare bedroom. I'm not sure how we did it in that tiny apartment. We were on top of each other, but we made it work for three years until my daughter remarried."*
> Carmen is a fifty-nine-year-old single grandmother.

now, as it is for older adult children and parents who have had financial or personal setbacks.

Finding Space

Families make the physical arrangements work by adding bunk beds, creating makeshift walls with room dividers, transforming the dining room into a bedroom, or by converting the garage into living or sleeping space. Those who have the means and enough property put on an addition to accommodate parents

> ## What Your Adult Child May Be Thinking
>
> *"I live with my dad. I clean the apartment, but he's a psycho clean freak. I'm the opposite. If there's something on the floor, I'll eventually get around to picking it up. I moved from my own apartment, and it's a struggle to get used to having a "roommate," especially because he's my dad, and compulsive."*
> Laura, twenty-three, lives with her father for the first time since she was six, when her parents divorced.

or in-laws. Some just pick up and buy or rent a larger apartment or house in order to fit everyone. When you want (or have) to be with family, you find the space.

When you want (or have) to be with family, you find the space.

Francine's daughter, son-in-law, and three grandchildren occupy the lower level of her home. Her daughter bought the furniture and her mother allows her to decorate any way she wants. "I had my office in an alcove off the boiler room and moved out my things so my son-in-law could use it as his office," Francine explains. "I took over my son's bedroom, who had moved out. We play 'musical rooms' in this house."

Julia, fifty-one, moved her mother into her home because none of her siblings wanted or could live with her. Julia, who is divorced, can't afford a large-enough house for everyone to have her own room, so she shares one bedroom with her mother and her two children have the other bedroom. "It will have to do," says Julia, "until I can afford a bigger place. Before he died, my father said he wanted her to live with me, and I have to honor his last wish."

WELCOME HOME

You want to make new arrivals feel at home, but you also don't want to be running a hotel for inconsiderate "boarders" who have no respect for your property. With younger adult children who return home, it's a good idea to spell out your house-keeping expectations. When Gordon's twenty-six-year-old son came home after a two-year relationship didn't work out,

Gordon told him that he had to keep his room clean. "It's a room in our house. He needs to contribute to maintaining this household."

Most everyone who lives on his or her own even for a short period of time develops his own way of keeping house. When someone moves into your home, your methods may go by the wayside. You can learn to ignore a messy room or a trail of belongings that don't quite make it to that messy room. Some things you can tolerate; for those you can't, you will have to communicate your wishes or relax your standards as a welcoming gesture.

Frequently, those moving in strive to be perfect "guests." A daughter-in-law, for instance, may feel obligated to clean up every minuscule Lego piece her children played with that day, even though she's bone-tired from a full day at work. To make her feel she's more a part of the family, tell her she doesn't have to straighten up every night, or offer to help her as you'd probably assist a daughter. Another way to encourage inclusion with those not related to you by blood is to ask for their help: hanging a picture, explaining how a new electronic device operates, sweeping out the garage, planting new shrubs, cooking dinner with or for you . . . When you treat the people married to your children—or, if you are the adult child, your in-laws—like family, feeling comfortable will come. The whole family will adjust more quickly if those moving in believe they are wanted.

The whole family will adjust more quickly if those moving in believe they are wanted.

Returning young adults may find their rooms just as they left them—posters still on the walls, high school notebooks and papers in the bookcase. Depending on an adult child's age, there's some risk in leaving the room completely intact. "My room was exactly the way I left it twenty years ago—a corkboard crammed with my high school and college stuff, softball mitt on a shelf, and Cabbage Patch dolls neatly positioned on the bed," says Marina, thirty-seven. "On seeing my room and the dolls, more than one date said, 'You've got to be kidding.' "

Other young adults may find their rooms bear no resemblance to the ones they grew up in. The room they called their own could have morphed into an office, sewing room, or a little sister's bedroom. Whether sons and daughters come home alone, or with a spouse and perhaps a child or two, they will appreciate the effort that went into making the room, or the one down the hall, theirs again.

Find memorabilia—a trophy, a favorite childhood object or a piece of sporting equipment, family photos—that's been stored in boxes or drawers, and take it out to display. Familiar touches make it much easier, like putting on a cozy sweater or worn sneakers, to feel as if you are truly home again.

When Linda, sixty, returned to live with her mother, she felt it was her mother's house, and she shouldn't bring her furniture and paraphernalia. "This is not my place; I'm not going to put anything of mine here. All I really needed to make it feel like home was pictures of my daughters in my room."

HOW TO WELCOME NEW ARRIVALS

- Hang a welcome home sign.
- Announce, "This is your home as well as ours now."
- Be inclusive by inviting "newcomers" to join you for the movies or dinner.
- Ease up on demands for orderliness.
- Ask them to pitch in and tell them how.
- Within your home's physical limitations, allow items that make it feel more like the home they came from.

Making Room

Putting out the welcome mat requires more than hanging a sign and saying "Glad you are here." Parents and in-laws and married and divorced adult children who have had their own homes may also feel a bit like intruders. They miss the place they used to call "home." Until everyone adapts to the new arrangement, "home" for them may remain the location they came from, the one with their furniture and their pictures on the walls. "You miss your belongings when what you had in your home is in storage or stashed in boxes in the garage. It feels weird," says Sophia, who moved in with her mother and stepfather.

Pamela went into creative problem-solving mode when she moved her seventy-two-year-old mother into her Chicago apartment. The problem: not nearly enough closet space. She gave her mother her bedroom and she slept in the tiny room with no closet in her small apartment. She put racks up in the dining area to hold her clothes, and they stayed there for the next ten years. "Having my things out in the open was worth it," she says, "because I didn't have to worry about financing two apartments, or my mother being alone."

When Helen's divorced daughter moved in after almost three decades of marriage, she had accumulated far more than Helen had room for, and most of it wasn't Helen's style or taste. Nonetheless, her daughter delights in displaying her artifacts from her travels around the globe. "My idea of decorating and art is having pictures of my children and grandchildren on the walls," Helen says. "Now I walk into a room and am startled by sculptures and paintings of African witch doctors on the walls and mounds of strange jewelry on her dresser. She sees this stuff as treasures, and I've learned to live with it."

Feeling at home calls for an ample dose of compromise on everyone's part when it comes to possessions—those already in place, and those coming in. An adult child out in the world for a few years may have an apartment full of furniture. Even if she leaves the furniture behind, as Stephanie did, the amount of belongings can still be sizable. "I went from an apartment to a room in a house, and there's no space for everything. After four years at home, I still have things in boxes, and if I leave something somewhere in the rest of the

Feeling at home calls for an ample dose of compromise on everyone's part when it comes to possessions.

house, my mother throws it into my room and shuts the door. That doesn't make me feel as if she wants me here."

Unpacking or weeding out your things will help ease tensions around the too-much-stuff problem. When a college graduate returns to reclaim his room, parents are often shocked by how much a young person owns, a good portion of which was probably paid for by his parents. It can feel as if your child has taken over again, absorbing every inch of space. The dresser, extra computer printer, plates, and paraphernalia from the apartment he shared with roommates at school get crammed into any available space, collecting dust. They are a constant reminder that this child is home to stay for a while. The stored items are not nearly as crucial as the personal changes that make adult conversation and exchanging ideas possible.

COMBINING TWO HOUSEHOLDS

If the returnee has been or is married, or are your parents or in-laws, you're likely to be looking at merging two complete households. Steel yourself for compromise, particularly if you're faced with a hoarder. After fifty-two years of marriage, Dawn's newly widowed mother dismantled her home in order to live with Dawn. "Mom asked if we could put a storage unit on my property, but I'm afraid to give her too much space because she has a real problem with collecting and saving. I believe if you're away from what you own, you don't miss it. My mother hasn't mentioned any of it. It's a good thing because my brother sold most it."

As an acquisitive society, we all have too much "stuff." Whoever is moving in will arrive with lots of baggage (literally). If you're putting yours into storage or squeezing it into an already-cluttered home, you may want to adopt the notion that possessions are only things. Ultimately, you can live without a painting, a souvenir from decades ago, or a cozy, but worn easy chair.

Brutal practicality, with a strong nod to sentimentality, around the things you and family members cherish is an approach that will minimize disagreement. You'll want to be as objective as possible about a coffee table or canister set or anything that duplicates what is already in the house. As you pare down, you'll also want to be sensitive to the divorced or jobless adult child who has suffered a terrible blow, or the parent who has recently lost a spouse and may be trying to hold on to objects that evoke memories of their marriage. Items that appear meaningless to you may not be to their owner. Be thoughtful as you make decisions about what to keep and what to discard.

Items that appear meaningless to you may not be to their owner.

Most homes can't hold two living-room couches or more beds and dressers than are already there. Assess the condition: Consider what's old, what's tattered, what looks and fits best as a first elimination step. Difficult as it is to imagine when you're in the thick of sorting through these belongings, you may be content to live with furniture or a salad bowl that is "new" to you.

Elizabeth doesn't see it that way. Her fifty-year-old daughter moved in four months ago with her husband and daughter and lots of packing cartons. "We're still digging our way out of all her stuff," Elizabeth grumbles. "We have duplicate kitchen equipment, dishes, and assorted household items I just don't need. I have it all." Elizabeth should consider looking over what she has and getting rid of chipped dishes and frayed blankets to reduce the clutter and make room for some of her daughter's things.

For a lot of people, the "things" are the least of it. Elizabeth's daughter also arrived with a pet bird and a large dog. You may be moving in with or welcoming a canary, parrot, cat, or dog, fish or gerbils—or any combination thereof—along with your parent, in-law, adult child, grandchildren, or sibling. It's a tough call if you're not fond of animals, or gave up having them when your last pet died. For some it's a major concession; for others, it's a no-brainer: Family includes their pets, and that's the way it is. Being in the "Pets Allowed" group says you respect your relative's feeling. Like many other aspects of living under the same roof again, you can stipulate what rooms pets may roam, who feeds them, and who cleans up after them.

SHARING SPACE

If left up in the air, indecisiveness about the use of rooms and equipment can become unnecessary irritants. Many parents I spoke with had had their adult children move in and move out, only to return again. The second or third time around, they say that they were smarter about situations that irked them the first time. They made rules about television shows—"If my daughter watches upstairs with me, I pick the shows"—and parking space—"I park in the driveway, my children have to park by the curb," to name a few.

You can also make sharing space tolerable by changing your attitude or cordoning off certain areas. "I thought they would be much neater than they are," Rita says of her daughter's family, who moved in a few years ago. "They know they can leave the upstairs a mess, but downstairs, except for the den, belongs to my husband and me. I had to enforce that rule because my husband can't stand disorder. Upstairs is theirs to do with as they please."

You might not love sharing a bathroom with adolescent grandsons. It can be terribly annoying at times, but those who share bathrooms must adapt, or try to think differently about the inconveniences and utter lack of regard for others who have to use the same bathroom. In the case of the grandsons in question, Grandma Joan complains: "They lose the cap to the toothpaste the first day it's opened, and that's the kindest thing I have to say about my grandsons and the deplorable state of the bathroom. I clean up a bit and look the other way, because everything else about living with them is such fun."

Bathroom etiquette can be more of a problem than you would think. You could be the only male in the house, jockeying for a bathroom perpetually occupied by one of the three females living with you. Twenty-six-year-old Kate shares a bathroom with two slightly younger brothers, and has well-founded objections: "Do you have any idea how disgusting guys are? I feel as if I live at a wilderness campground. I don't step in the bathroom or shower without sandals on my feet."

The one room that everyone shares, regardless of how spacious the home or how many bathrooms, is the kitchen. Two women in one kitchen is generally not conducive to maintaining warm, caring relationships. I know this firsthand from watching my grandmother and mother share the kitchen. For two months every summer, we lived with my father's parents. I could count on seeing my mother in tears fairly often around dinnertime. My grandmother had to do things her way, and we all had to follow her lead. As a kid, I did what I was told, but I knew preparing meals under my grandmother's critical eye was torture for my mother.

Some people find sharing the kitchen near impossible. To alleviate the tension, they assign kitchen privileges at set hours for each "chef" in the house. Others eat takeout to avoid cooking conflicts. For all those who can't get along in the kitchen, there's an equal number who enjoy cooking with their adult children, parents, or in-laws.

WHAT'S MINE IS MINE ... AND YOURS

There's a level of respect the adults in the house need to adopt; it extends from cleaning up and leaving a space shipshape for others, to caring for property that isn't yours. In short, what's mine is yours—to a point. As the homeowner, you have the right to demand respect for the things you worked hard to buy. Your children aren't young anymore, and insisting they take care of what is yours is more than reasonable. The same holds true for parents or in-laws who move in with you. If you're doing the cooking in your mother or mother-in-law's home, you'd better be leaving the kitchen sparkling for her or the next person who will be at the stove. Vacuum the rooms your children play in, and pull the vacuum into common areas in the house without being asked.

Do your own laundry, and find out if anyone else has things they would like washed. Without common courtesy, use of the laundry room, like other communal appliances and space, can become a grating issue. Marilyn (the homeowner) was forced to arrange a schedule with her two over-thirty-year-old children. Instead of having first choice, she had to wait until her adult children had finished their wash before she could do hers and her husband's. When you've been living together for a long time, the lines can get cloudy, as Marilyn notes. "My children think they should be able to do their chores when they want to, and that I need to adjust to them, rather than them adjusting to me."

SOME PRIVACY, PLEASE

Perhaps the biggest adjustment is the change in the amount of privacy everyone has. Privacy is hard to come by in a full house, or one that feels full. Not so long ago you were on your own, out of the sight of close relatives. Lack of privacy—giving it and getting it—is a real issue for parents, as well as their adult children, especially when sharing a small apartment or house. It can begin to feel as if you have no privacy. Amanda, who works long hours, knows the

Lack of privacy— giving it and getting it—is a real issue.

problem well. "We live in a smaller home. Sometimes I like being alone, but there's always someone there. When I come home, my parents ask questions about my day, and I don't want to talk. I've been talking all day at the hospital."

If you're not working, those you live with see what you do all day. The closer the quarters, the easier it is for family members to be in each other's "business." Everyone should make an effort to back off a bit and give each other emotional room when physical space is not an option. Ask fewer questions and allow some time for unwinding. If you are the one in need of quiet time, excuse yourself and go to your room to be alone.

If you work from home, there's the possibility that your routine will need altering to accommodate your parents or adult children. Space is at a premium in Elaine's apartment, and she's tucked her office in an alcove between her two children's bedrooms. That worked well before her two adult children returned to live with her. When one of them has an overnight guest, Elaine is torn between wanting to get to work first thing in the morning and wanting to give her offspring some privacy. "If I go to my computer," she says, "I feel as if I'm being intrusive. That's just too awkward for me. Instead, I use that time to run errands or work on projects that don't require the computer, until everyone is awake."

Married couples living with their parents or in-laws face similar privacy problems. Nina and her husband moved back into her childhood home and bedroom about a year after their wedding. "My husband never complained, but for sure it was uncomfortable with my parents' bedroom down the hall," reveals Nina. "There was not much of anything going on in our bedroom for the couple years we lived with them."

Unless the walls are made of concrete, or there's ample separation between occupied bedrooms, it's also more difficult to fight with your partner when you live with family. When parents or adult children are arguing, consider moving to a spot from which you can't hear what is being said. Stay out of personal disagreements you may overhear. If someone wants your input, he'll ask for it. Backing off and not interfering helps achieve some semblance of privacy in a home with paper-thin walls or limited space.

There's No Place Like Home

As much as family enjoys having its members close at hand, most people recognize the desire to be alone, or alone with one's partner and children. Yet, in the majority of families, as soon as space is allocated and personal items are in place, it begins to feel like home to all who live there. "We tease that they are never going to move out," says Rita of her daughter and her family. "We are all so content, but I know eventually it's better for them if they have their own home for their growing family."

If it's your place, there will be times when you want your space back, or if you've moved in, a place to call your own. David's position: "It would be nice to know that my sons are independent," he says, "and I had more of the house to do the things I want to do."

Until then, David and others who are living together again have to reorient themselves to sharing bathrooms, living with animals not their own, and having less privacy than they had before. But, when all is said and done, few end up disgruntled about the changes. In fact, they believe it was more than worth it, no matter what they had to alter.

Joyce certainly feels that way about her twenty-six-year-old son's return: "I had a difficult time when my children left home to go to college, but I got used to life without them. It's so nice to be close to Jeffrey again. That outweighs the inconveniences."

LIVING LIKE PEAS IN A POD

- Abandon any notion of how you think sharing a house will be.
- Look the other way as much as you can.
- Be less intrusive.
- Be courteous and respectful of everyone's property.
- Clean up after yourself and your young children.
- Don't take advantage of the comforts being provided.

Chapter Seven

Together and Apart

EVEN IF THE LIVING SPACE IS GRAND OR PRIVATE, FAMILY MEMBERS need time away from each other. Before your offspring or parents or in-laws crossed the threshold again (or you crossed theirs), you had a life very different from four or thirty-four years ago, when you had the responsibility of raising—or answering to—family. Free of those constraints, you constructed a life around your interests and pursued them more or less at will. You went out with friends or had them to your house, shopped all day, ventured off for long runs or bike rides, played a sport or exercised on your schedule. Time away from those you live with helps frame your identity and brings novel ideas and more interesting conversation back to the family.

When you live with a relative again, what you do and when you do it can become less certain. You might feel obligated to spend your free time with them—or worse, feel responsible for their happiness, definitely a preventable burden. Happiness is a solo achievement; no one can make someone else happy by being with or available to them all the time. We've all heard this and know it objectively; acting on it is a different story.

I don't care who you are, how compatible or how significant the adjustments you've made to establish boundaries, being together 24/7 is a prescription for

Being together 24/7 is a prescription for troublesome relationships.

troublesome relationships. Be it your twenty-something or forty-something, your seventy-five-year-old TV junkie mom, or your rock-climbing in-law, you really can have too much of a good thing. You have lived by yourself or with a roommate, partner, or spouse, and had a taste of being free—free from any former role you had in the family. And now, coming back to live with a parent or adult child, it can feel as if you were never apart. You can begin to feel as if you are no longer a separate person, as if you melded right back into your former role of vigilant parent or mama or dad's dutiful daughter or son standing at your parent's side.

You want a life you can claim as your own—validation that you are a distinct person, not so intertwined with a parent or child that you have trouble deciphering where you begin and he or she ends. By spending too much time together, you can begin to feel like an identical twin whose parent dressed you alike and people could not tell you apart. You were inseparable and did most everything together. Later in life, one or both twins will likely have great difficulty conjuring up an identity unique from their look-alike sibling.

Once patterns and expectations are established, it can feel hard, if not impossible, to change them. That's why it's important as soon as you notice a problem—or before—to assert your independence and act on it. Imagine you live with your mother who does your laundry, has dinner on the table every night, keeps house efficiently, and the garden weeds in check. You are a spoiled grown-up and you recognize it. What's not to like? You share a heaping bowl of popcorn when you watch a movie and shop together, same as you did when you were a teenager. Lovely that you get along so famously, but you will eventually

> ## What Your Parent May Be Thinking:
>
> *"I feel like I'm stuck. I gear my cooking to them and feel obligated to have dinner with them every night. We see friends less and eat out less."*
>
> Nancy, sixty-four, is the mother of two daughters (ages thirty-four and thirty-nine) who both live at home.

get on each other's nerves. Petty annoyances that you prefer not to acknowledge or try to push out of your mind will loom larger if you don't have time away from each other.

If you are the parent or grandparent, out of habit, you're at the ready to be helpful and available. It's what you have done your entire adult life. It may take another person's schedule, or insistence, to get you to grasp that they have things to do that don't include you. You may be forced to "let them go." Or, hopefully, you realize yourself that they and you need some separation.

> ## What Your Adult Child May Be Thinking
>
> *"Moving home after living in another city, I worried about my parents wanting me around and not being able to have my own social circle."*
>
> Amanda, twenty-five, hadn't lived in her hometown since she was eighteen.

SEPARATE LIVES

In conversation, Nancy refers to herself as the "slave" to her husband and daughters, and falls into the trap of letting her guilt and love for her family interfere with her needing to get on with her life. She rationalizes clinging to parenting by saying, "We like each other. We feel more complete when we're all together."

A few times a year, Nancy leaves her husband and daughters to fend for themselves while she visits an older son, daughter-in-law, and grandchildren in another state, but that's not enough to break the cycle and regain her and her husband's once-active social life. Interestingly, her younger daughter is aware of the need to separate and travels most weekends to be with friends who follow the women's golf circuit. Like Nancy's daughter, recent college grads and other young adult children who focus on their social lives have less difficulty carving out a life that is not completely governed by family.

One of the major hazards for parents whose adult children return home is expecting to be with them, waiting to make plans until their children firm up theirs, or, worse, giving up what they enjoy based on the possibility (and often it's quite remote) that their children will be around. Adult children, on the other hand, hopefully put all their time and energy into making contacts with old and new friends, and trying to get their adult lives in order. Amanda met new people, made friends, and, as she says, "I was able to start over." Most parents are not the top priority at this juncture in their young adult children's lives.

When you move in with parents with whom you are compatible, who are undemanding or make your life effortless, it can also happen that you find yourself relying on them too much and spending time with them almost exclusively. In a complete turnabout, Nina, twenty-nine, who shared an apartment with her husband before they moved in with her parents, discloses how their life changed. "When Dan and I lived in our apartment, we had friends over every Friday night. We were pretty much the only couple with an apartment; we were young, and most of our friends still lived with their parents. Ours was the place to meet and party. Once we were with my parents, they became the couple we hung out with. We didn't go out much and saw less and less of friends. We both loved living there, and my parents made it so easy. I'm not sure if that was good or bad."

Sharing and togetherness are admirable—to a point. If you are the parent, single or married, with a young adult back in your home, arrange to spend plenty of time with your own peers. Your offspring can have all the respect in the world for you and enjoy being with you, but you are still the parent. You are no longer in that young groove. Don't try to act as if you are, tempting though it may be. Having youth around the house will keep you vital and tuned in to what their generation is thinking, but, with a few exceptions (like Nina), you are probably not their companion of choice. Suzanne confirms this when she says of her twenty-nine-year-old resident son, "We might go out to eat on occasion, but we don't hang out together."

Ian, thirty-three, likes the fact that his relationship with his parents is less of the domineering parent-child type he experienced growing up, but says, "I only socialize with them a bit. If I know their friends, I'll join them, but if I don't, I avoid the situation unless asked. My feeling is that since I'm living here, I don't want to disrupt their lives any more than I already do."

Most parents don't want to rearrange their lives to be Mom and Dad again. Keep commitments and social engagements in much the same way you did before the "boomerang." Don't change dates to accommodate an adult child who may cancel plans with you at a moment's notice—a habit for which twenty-somethings are famous. Your young adult is perfectly able to come home to an empty house, prepare dinner, and amuse himself or entertain friends.

Most parents don't want to rearrange their lives to be Mom and Dad again.

Believe it or not, just when you think your adult children will never leave, they do. You don't want to be in the position of having to re-create your social life again. Margery is an old hand at having adult children come home; at different points, all three of her adult children returned, the older two when they were out of college and working. Her third son, in his early forties, arrived with his wife and babies after selling his home and looking to buy another—a process which took several years. On the subject of returning children, Margery has it right when she says, "We did not change our lives because our kids were here. They conformed to us."

As the "move-in" family member, just how much conforming do you need to do? Who goes out and how often doesn't have to be an issue, nor should it be, as long as everyone is considerate. Give notice when you have plans to allow others in the family to make their own if they wish.

CARVING OUT TIME

It is clear from talking to adult children and parents that those who take a breather from each other on a fairly regular basis, and those who have interests beyond family, have fewer problems living together. Being in the same house means being with family a good portion of each day, and any free time you had can quickly evaporate. In any twenty-four-hour period, so many hours are committed to working or looking for work, preparing meals and all that goes into that, and maintaining the house that not many are left over for pleasure anyway. For some, being away from family is automatic: They travel for their jobs, go off to see other relatives regularly, or have commitments made long before their living situation changed.

Ann is the first to acknowledge that living with her mother works because she is often gone for a month or two at a time in Europe, on archaeological digs for work. Of her time away, she says, "My siblings are close by and they step up, stop by, or do things with Mom when I'm away. It's a good break for both of us."

Smaller breaks are just as therapeutic. You may have a family member who prepares dinner every night, but that doesn't mean you always have to eat together. That's particularly significant when an offspring's entire family lives with you. Your son and his family might do takeout one night and you eat leftovers whenever you get hungry. Even though family dinners provide many benefits, in expanded families, time alone or with friends is refreshing, especially if you engage in activities you enjoy.

Francine, who has a high-pressure job in a staid Wall Street firm, is an unlikely candidate for spending her free-from-family time selling sex paraphernalia. A few times a month she leads all-female parties and has a great time. "At first everyone in my house was against my signing up to be a sex-toys sales representative, but I knew I needed to be away from the house and the people in it. I've been hosting women-only parties for three years, and I love the laughs. For me, it's the perfect outlet for the craziness that goes on with energetic grandchildren, their parents, and my husband. It's extra money and harmless amusement for a woman my age." Francine is fifty-four.

Francine's pick may not be yours, but it is only one of thousands of possibilities that get you away from the routine, tension, or stress at home. You may favor a book club that reads only the classics, or a group that trains for a marathon. You might like a weekly or monthly dinner with girlfriends, a regular poker game, or to watch a televised sporting event now and then with friends in a bar. Make the effort; the good feeling you will have is immeasurable.

It's not mandatory to have to ask permission or to explain yourself either. Evelyn's twenty-something grandson currently lives in her former rec room that over the years has been occupied by some of her four children and their wives and offspring. She makes a valid point: "I learned not to tell everyone exactly what I was going to do. I believe you should live your life as you want. It's my life. I let them know that if they want me, I'm here, but they don't have to know where I'm going all the time. In my house, we live together, but basically apart."

GIVE YOURSELF A BREAK

Not everyone separates so easily from their adult children, especially parents who move in with you. Frequently they don't necessarily want a life independent of yours, and are hesitant or obstinate about pursuing one. Kimberly's parents were married for almost fifty years, and they both worked and had little time for friends. Their free time was spent together. When her mother died, her father was retired and at a loss without his companion. He looked to Kimberly, forty-three, to fill the void and his time. After much prodding on Kimberly's part, he made a life for himself by joining a reading club, getting involved with church programs, and finding people with whom to exercise. "He really had to find a substitute for me since I'm away on business at least one week a month. He seems happy now," says Kimberly, "so I don't worry about him so much."

Taking breaks may require rigorous planning and persistence. Start by telling a mother- or father-in-law with whom you've spent weeks or months helping adjust to life in your home that you will be going out on Thursday for the evening, or to a yoga class on Wednesday afternoons. The next week you might add another outing to the list. Slowly, the transition to your being gone for a few hours will sink in. If getting out of the house means turning over responsibility to someone else in the family, don't be shy. Find a sibling, aunt, uncle, or one of your older children to fill in for you. Lean on a friend if you have to.

Taking breaks may require rigorous planning and persistence.

Parents living with adult children need friends and a social life to circumvent depression and other health risks, as well as to avoid casting a pall over the entire household. When Karen's mother was fifty-five, she lived with Karen; unfortunately, she stayed in her room all day, watching television. She eventually left at her daughter's urging. "I told her she should be out making a great life for herself after the struggle of raising me and my siblings," says Karen. "She deserved it. I had a hard time watching her wasting herself. I couldn't budge her even after explaining that it hurt me to see her that way. I said, 'You're not being part of my life or making one for yourself.' " Her mother moved to another state near extended family, returning to live with Karen again ten years later.

When you know a parent's living with you is permanent, there's greater incentive to establish connections and resources for him or her. Julia goes to church with her mother and takes her to exercise classes in hopes that she will meet people and make friends. "My mother is basically lazy and satisfied to be with me and the children. Whatever I'm doing, my mother wants to do. That drives me crazy. I need to get away from her sometimes."

Not being dependent on family for your entire social life opens new vistas and, for people like Francine, provides some good fun. But, if you have a dependent parent or adult child, wanting time to yourself can set off arguments or quiet brooding. Getting time to yourself becomes your needs versus the needs of those you live with. The healthy decision is to free yourself from an expectant or problematic adult child, parent, or in-law.

**ALTERING PATTERNS OF
TOO MUCH TOGETHERNESS**

- Make changes in small steps.
- Give advance notice of when you will be out, followed by stipulating all the times you will be home and available.
- Cut down on one-to-one time even when you are home.
- Set a clingy relative on a path of being on his or her own by doing the investigating for him or her.
- Go so far as planning something for your dependent relative to do if that's what it takes to jump-start a more independent life.

BUILDING SOCIAL NETWORKS

For the most part, those moving into a parent's, adult child's, or sibling's home are relocating to a new area, or back to where they grew up and have maintained few, if any of their old friends. In essence, you or they are "all dressed up," wanting to make a new life, but having nowhere to go and no one to go with. With a bit of exploring, you can build relationships outside the family for yourself or for those in your family who need them.

If you've moved back into your childhood neighborhood, renew your ties by calling former friends. On reunion, high school, and college Web sites, you can find out where your classmates might be. Maybe one or two stayed local. Attend (or encourage your adult child or parent to attend) a reunion even in an "off" year. You are just as likely to make a connection at a ninth or twelfth reunion as you are at a twentieth or fiftieth.

If someone in your family seems at a loss about what to do, have a conversation to discover what he or she might be interested in and want to pursue. There may be a lifelong goal of learning Spanish or how to swim or make pottery that was never revealed. Once you have an inkling, talk to people in line at the grocery store or in shops you frequent to find out if they know about a group or organization that might fit a mentioned preference. Although there are many others, here are some ideas for getting involved:

- Watch for posters in store windows announcing events that may spark interest.

- Read the messages on grocery store bulletin boards.

- Check out activities affiliated with religious groups.

- Sign up for a course at a community college or a night course at the local high school.

- Attend musical performances or bookstore readings.

- Join a gym, or a bridge, book, or chess club.

- Volunteer at an animal shelter, the hospital, or with a political activist group.

- Search the Internet to find just what you may be looking for.

These are viable starting points for getting out and about, living life. Reserve blocks of time for yourself, or you will not be able to carve out the personal or alone time you need and deserve. A change of scene broadens horizons and breaks the cycle that at times could feel as if it's strangling you.

When you're apart, you each have your own space and time to revitalize. Ruth carries a heavy load caring for her daughter's family while her daughter and son-in-law go to work. In her mid-seventies, she feels the strain of not getting away from her family responsibilities. "It's not only taking care of my grand-children; it's all the relatives who stop in—and want dinner—as if they had never seen babies before."

After months of nonstop housework and cooking, Ruth's son offered his log cabin in the mountains. Ruth and her hus-band used it one weekend. "I didn't want to do anything. It was as if I had been let out of prison. I just sat in a chair and read and watched TV. I need a weekend to myself every so often," she reports.

It almost doesn't matter what you do. Going off on your own protects relationships—and your sanity. Separateness has an essential place in family life and will help retain good feel-ings for the long haul. Although it's reassuring to have the com-pany and companionship of *Going off on your own protects relationships—and your sanity.* family, breaks from each other are mentally, if not physically, invigorating. You—or your loved ones—will be a happier per-son who is better able to cope with the complications that come with living under the same roof again.

Chapter Eight

The Dating Life

Friends and lovers can be as much a part of life for twenty-two-year-olds as they are for eighty-year-olds. Divorced parents and adult children find new mates; widows and widowers start anew; the never-married meet the person of their dreams. When dating and sex lives are factored into the family formula, conflicting feelings are easy to come by. However, by learning to trust that your parent or adult child will use good judgment, and by honoring his or her choices, dating and romance can be a joyous part of family life. When family is receptive to new romantic attachments, everyone wins; sharing good times, new experiences, and different points of view make family life more interesting.

Dating and romance can be a joyous part of family life.

Dating dilemmas and your feelings about a mother or father or adult child's comments and attitude are real, and should be acknowledged. That's the first step in getting your family to view the situation differently. Having members of the household date might feel threatening if you believe they are involved with the "wrong" person, or if you thought they would never be with anyone again in a romantic sense.

The arrival of a new person poses difficulties if you or the family you live with has visions for your life together remaining as it is. You could also worry about your loss of status, or

---

What Your Parent May Be Thinking

"When my daughter lost her job a year ago, she moved in with me and my live-in partner. He's quiet, not out-going or funny like her father. Lily steers clear of him and did even when he and I were dating. I wish she would accept that I love this man and make more of an effort to talk to him. That would make me happy."

Gina, sixty-four, divorced for twelve years, has shared her home with her live-in boyfriend for three years, and with her thirty-year-old daughter for one year.

---

how to incorporate a new person into the family "structure," as Helen does. "My daughter is divorced and in her fifties, way too young to be celibate, yet I worry that she will meet someone and move him into the house. I would feel I have to leave after living here fifty years."

The complexities of dating don't escape those much younger either. You could worry about your parents loving the guy or gal you love, or, contrarily, you could have sworn off dating having recently left a bad relationship, or had one that ended in a messy, drawn-out divorce. In the latter instance,

---

What Your Adult Child May Be Thinking:

"I have to sacrifice my relationship with my boyfriend by seeing him less. I don't discuss him around my parents because they don't approve. It's the one trouble spot with my parents, but it's a big one."

Rebecca, twenty-eight, has lived with her parents for the last six years.

---

your parents or child constantly urge you to see other people. You're not remotely ready to entertain the idea of a social life, but that doesn't stop the nudging. In time, your position could change and you could find yourself wanting to date again. Love is unpredictable at any age . . . and how family reacts, more so.

FRIENDS AND LOVERS

In the best of all worlds, you accept whomever your parent or adult child dates or moves in. You're "all ears" for the positive details, as well as the gripes and concerns. You listen to projections about the future or the hopelessness of continuing the relationship. As you would with a good friend, you celebrate the positives or you advise, and your suggestions are respected, if not always followed. That's what you hope will happen, but too often, it doesn't. In their concern for your happiness or their own significance in your life, family falls prey to their own idea of how things should be. Those closest to you can become cautious, like Lily; stubborn, confrontational, even dictatorial—sometimes rightly so. In other situations, they are wrong to the detriment of the bond they have with their adult child or parent.

Karen's mother behaves in ways that gravely alarm Karen. She feels justified in her reactions because her mother lives with her. Her formerly shut-in mother is, ten years later, a hip sixty-five with dating as her only interest. Her daughter labeled her mother a "male magnet" because men stop the car and there's an instant connection through the windshield, Karen tells me. "My big issue is that my mother is overly private. When she meets a guy, she doesn't tell us who he is or where she's going. My sister and I want to know where to look for the dead body if she doesn't return.

"I know that some of the men my mother's involved with are married. I haven't met them and don't want to. I ask her what is it about her feelings of self-worth that let her go out with men who are unavailable. I don't want my five-year-old seeing her grandmother with married men. I really believe she enjoys the drama of me saying you cannot bring married men here. I don't respect or appreciate that sort of relationship."

Although Karen wants her mother to date and get out of the house, she tacks on one more thing about her mother's dating that bothers her: "It's creepy that younger men in their forties are attracted to her—they're my age."

Ordinarily you would peg that comment as jealousy. Not so in Karen's case, but it can be in other mother-daughter duos, with jealousy stemming from either party. If you're feeling sorry for yourself when your parent or adult child is on a date or in a serious relationship, rethink how you feel. Weigh what you say to avoid sounding competitive with your "dating" relative. Be willing to share your parent, son, daughter, or sibling, and be understanding of a new friend or lover's demands that reduce your time together.

Weigh what you say to avoid sounding competitive with your "dating" relative.

Adult Children, Single and Dating

Because you know your parents well, you can be prepared to handle problems that might surface. Let's face it: When you live at home, a parent has more opportunities to know the personal details of your life, particularly if you decide to share them.

Eric, thirty, has lived with his parents in one- and two-year stretches since graduating from college. He opts to tell his mother about the women he dates, but, as you might expect, divulging can have residual consequences. Eric shares some personal details with his mother, but even if he didn't, living with a parent automatically gives her more access to information. "My mom has always been worried about my romances," he says. "If I tell her my longtime girlfriend and I had a fight, she tells me she's a great gal and I shouldn't screw it up. So much for siding with your child—but that doesn't bother me. I know in the end, she'll support me. Now she just wants me to get married."

Unlike Eric, others feel their parents are way too intrusive. Those who choose to keep their romantic lives to themselves disclose little about their comings and goings. With respect to including his parents in his social life, Jim hasn't wavered from the tactic he used at age eighteen. "I don't say who, or how many times I've seen someone. I'm fifty and still sneaking around. It seems easier than facing the questions I know will come."

The Grilling Begins
The inquisitive parent at full throttle sounds something like this: "Who are you going out with? Where did you meet? How long have you known her? What does he do? How often are you

seeing her? What's he like? When are you bringing her home to meet us?" A more-subtle parent might say, "So what did you do last night?" Less pointed, but still seeking the same information.

Parents may not like the information they get. "My parents question the intentions of the man I've been seeing. They asked me if our relationship was just a physical one. They asked me if I saw a future with this person, and told me they didn't. After I reevaluated the romance and what my parents said, I concluded that mine and my parent's view are light years apart regarding the person I'm dating," says Rebecca, who refuses to end the relationship.

Only you can know when you are serious enough about someone to provide the particulars, or to have your parents meet him or her. Until then, urge your parent to stop prying. In order to get around personal interrogations,

---

You Might Say:

- "I know you want to know everything, but I'm not prepared to tell you."

- "I appreciate your interest, but stop the personal inquisition."

- "I'll answer two questions. Choose them carefully, because I'm counting."

- "Trust me, I'll tell all when I think I'm seeing someone you should know about."

- "It may turn into something, but it's not at the moment. I'll keep you posted."

Being Romantic

Even if you're willing to open up about your love life, the obstacles to being romantic when you live with your parents bring up more questions. You'll want to answer them before you spill out your heart to a parent. Suppose you meet someone at a party or on a blind date; are you willing to say "Come home with me to my parents' house"? Can you be relaxed and romantic with your parent in the next room? Can the person you're dating, love, or plan to marry spend the night?

FINDING UNINTERRUPTED DATE TIME

- Ask to have the house to yourself for an agreed-upon evening or weekend.
- Come up with a plan that doesn't inconvenience your parents and gives you time to have a romantic dinner or watch a movie.
- Drop a younger sibling off at the movies to eliminate unexpected interruptions in your evening, or embarrassing kid comments.
- Send your parents out to dinner "on you," if you can afford it.

SLEEPOVERS—POSSIBLE OR NOT?

With some parents, allowing dates to spend the night is a non-issue as long as it's not a virtual parade of different partners. Liberal-thinking parents go so far as to buy queen-sized beds for their adult offspring's rooms. Parents mildly opposed look the other way, while those strongly opposed put rules in place. If a rule has been instituted, as in Gordon's house, it needs to be observed. "When our son has a visitor, we vacate the television room and go to our bedroom or the study," reports Gordon, father of a twenty-six-year-old. "My wife and I draw the line at him taking women into his room and closing the door."

When rules or feelings are stated, it's difficult to go against parents' wishes. It is, after all, their house. "My parents were so sick of me dating losers, that when I found a responsible guy who was good to me, they allowed him to move into their home," Chloe, twenty-eight, explains. "But, my mother liking him wasn't enough to change her traditional views."

Chloe's mother was precise when she agreed to the new houseguest: "You're not close to married," she told her daughter. "You will sleep in separate rooms. I am not stupid, but I don't want it in my face. Sleeping together in a boldface way is disrespectful to me."

Rules about sexual encounters and sleeping over in a parent's home are often known, but unspoken. Parents' morals and values override any intentions an adult child might have. Kate, twenty-six, grew up in a very Christian Reformed family. She says, "Lots of things are extremely black and white with my parents, and ridden with guilt, produced by looks and little comments. My parents have strong opinions about things that don't make sense to me, and you know them without them saying a word. I've had the same boyfriend for several years, but my parents get distraught when I spend the night at his house.

"The family, my siblings, my boyfriend, and I are planning a camping trip. My dad made an announcement to no one in particular, but I know it was directed at me: 'No one can share tents with significant others.' That about sums it up. It's pretty clear: There's no way they'll let him sleep in my room at home. We never talk about these things, but we should.'"

Relaxing the No-Sleepover Rule

At some point the no-bed-sharing stipulation may turn impractical or feel unreasonable. Although you understand the need to honor parents' house rules, when you find yourself spending the night away from home or resorting to sneaking in and out of bedrooms, it may be time to start a dialogue. Here are some possible ways to relax the no-sleepover rule:

- Remind parents that you are a grown-up who lived independently and made good decisions before returning to live with them.

- Explain that restrictive "house rules" only serve to keep you away from them more than you would like.

- Bring up your safety by asking if they want you traveling alone in the early-morning hours, or driving after you've been drinking.

- Explain the seriousness of your relationship with the person with whom you would like to spend the night.

PARENTS DATING

With the divorce rate still hovering at 50 percent, it's very likely that your mother or father (or both) will have a new love interest while you are living together. Who would have thought that your mother would take a lover and flaunt him in front of you, or that your children would learn the facts of life from their grandmother? For many adult children, it's hard to fathom that their mother is sexually active, or that their father is seeing someone younger than they are. It's hard to be welcoming under such circumstances.

For reasons you don't quite grasp, a parent hooks up with someone who seems too flashy, too intellectual, or too interested in climbing the social ladder—or the opposite; in other words, a surprising match for your parent. You may also be dismayed if you feel the new person is assuming the role of your much-loved deceased or absent parent, or is taking over your role as watchful protector. It will be especially difficult to be amicable if you doubt a new partner's suitability or suspect he or she is after your parent's money.

Adjusting to a Parent's New Mate

The first step in warming to a parent's new partner is to figure out why you are hesitant to accept your parent's choice. Keep in mind: When you are not happy about the romantic person in your parent's life, your parent will probably be very torn between wanting to please you and wanting to hold on to the romance. The following may help you adjust to a parent's new mate:

- Give the new partner a chance.

- Try not to view this person as a parent figure; he or she is not displacing your other parent.

- Look for interests to share as a way to include a parent's new partner in the family.

- Don't be overly protective of your parent.

- Express serious objections or concerns delicately, but promptly.

- Don't endanger your children's relationship with a grandparent with negative comments about the person your parent loves.

- Recognize that a parent's choice of companion is not yours to make.

- Stay in groups to help dissipate difficult or awkward situations.

- Don't put your parent in the position of having to take sides or choose between you and a new partner.

- Make concessions if they will keep the bond to your parent strong.

Let go of dislikes and overlook small annoyances and shortcomings if your parent is happy. If need be, focus on the new partner's good points, and accept that cordiality may be the best you can achieve. You're an adult, too, who can make relatively minor alterations that will reflect your maturity and desire to maintain a mutually supportive connection. Being gracious takes so much less time and psychic energy than refusing to acknowledge the relationship or the person. You may indeed grow to like, even love, your parent's new dating partner, who may well be (or already is) a new housemate.

ANSWERING TO YOUR ADULT CHILD

Before you and your adult child joined forces to live together again, you may have dated as you wished, welcoming the freedom to go out with whomever you chose. A grown child's scrutiny of every man or woman you see socially can make having a love life difficult, or unpleasant at the very least, as it was for Gina with her daughter. If the relationship is worth holding on to and you think your adult child is off base in negating your preferences, you can ask her why she acts the way she does. You can also let your child know how you feel so he understands your position.

You Might Say or Ask:

- "What is the point of your attitude or behavior toward the person I'm seeing (or love)?"

- "Your behavior is not helping my relationship with him, or with you."

- "What do you hope to gain?"

- "Whom are you really punishing?"

- "Your attitude will not change my mind about the person I want to spend my time with."

EMOTIONS RUN DEEP ON BOTH SIDES

Often when you live together, parent and adult child wind up watching out for each other and becoming each other's sounding boards. They can complain about last night's date to a listener who truly cares. Intimate sharing can also lead to conflict.

Stephanie, thirty-one, returned home one evening to find one of her mother's ex-boyfriends sitting on the living-room sofa. After he left, Stephanie confronted her mother. Her position was that her mother broke up with this guy because he didn't treat her mother well. Stephanie had spent hours consoling her crying mother each time the man in question was rude or mean or heartless. "She came to me many times with mascara running down her face. I didn't want to see her hurt again, and told her so, but she came back at me with, 'You have no right to get involved.' "

There will probably be some upheaval and differences around dating and love issues, a protection of turf as Stephanie's mother sees it. When any family member acts inappropriately, such as the grandmother mentioned earlier who was being overtly sexual in front of her grandchildren, you'll want to speak up. As an adult child (or parent), you could say something like, "I know you like this person, and we're happy for you, but we have young children. Could you hold back on the displays in front of them?"

Proper and discreet behavior will stem much of the conflict. High on the "don't" list is having a string of different partners if you live with grandchildren. Children attach fairly easily and could be disappointed when a date is there and gone as quickly as he or she arrived. Let discretion and common sense dictate your actions.

Those who live together want to see their mother or father or son or daughter happy. Because emotions run deep, the best approach is one that is composed and empathetic when things aren't going well in the love department for your parent or adult child. You will be the most helpful if you pre-think what you want to say, even making notes of the key points you want to get across before you speak.

Because emotions run deep, the best approach is one that is composed and empathetic.

Controversy typically arises because both have a hoped-for mate in mind for their parent or adult children. Rarely is anyone quite good enough. Acceptance of another person's paramour usually comes with time, as you get to know each other and see what your parent or adult child saw in their significant other that at first you didn't.

THE NEW DYNAMICS

As you become more involved with someone and envision a change in how or where you will be living, give plenty of advance notice. You may reach the point at which your relationship can be classified as "committed," and you would like to move your significant other into the house. A discussion is a must. Perhaps one of the big advantages is the contribution, either financial or in the way of help, the new arrival will be able to make to the family. If you plan to move out so you can live together, prepare those you live with. You don't want to shock older parents who may feel you are abandoning them. And, you don't want to leave a family member in a financial lurch if you have been contributing to the support and running of the household.

IMPLEMENTING THE NEW DYNAMICS

- Be cautious and slow when introducing a new person to the family.
- Prepare them with positive information about the person you're dating.
- A frank talk is more likely to produce acceptance than is sneaking around or lying about where you're going or where you've been—and with whom.
- With a very opinionated or nosy relative, withhold facts that you know will provoke argument.
- Don't expect instantaneous adoration for the person you bring home.
- With any romantic involvements for parents or adult children, avoid a revolving door of mate after mate, night after night or month after month.
- If you are a parent looking to date, consider asking your adult children to introduce you to Internet dating.

Chapter Nine

Homeward Bound
at Twenty-Something

It used to be that parents wondered—and some still do—what they did wrong when their college graduates were not immediately independent. Rest assured, you didn't fail as a parent and your child didn't fail as an adult. Times have changed—and not favorably—for launching young adults into the world.

CollegeGrad.com conducted a survey in June of 2009, and found that 80 percent of college graduates moved home. That's an increase from the 77 percent in 2008 and 67 percent in 2006. Sixty-four and a half percent of the 2008 graduates said they would live home until they found a job, and 12.4 percent said they were moving home for the summer. Recent history indicates students' projections are unrealistic. The 2006 and 2007 graduates expected to live with family for six months, but have stayed for much longer periods. The migration to family and stays lasting for years are understandable given shrinking job opportunities, high housing costs, and students' inability to pay back loans while keeping up with car payments, cell-phone bills, and the luxuries to which they became accustomed as students.

Parents foot most, if not all, the bills for students not on full scholarship. Twenty-somethings grew up in a culture of yes-parenting. They were given what they wanted, or bought it themselves when times were flourishing and jobs were readily available. In high school parents are pretty much the source of everything children require. When their adult children return home after college, or being on their own for several years, parents can find themselves back in high school mode to the extent they allow it. A teenager's life centered around the house, and until the teen had a driver's license, he relied on his parents to get him to activities.

It's safe to say that parents hope their grown children will finish their educations, be employed, and live on their own. Typically, when baby boomers graduated from college, they found a job, a roommate, and housing shortly after graduation. They were expected to firm up plans and forge ahead, secure with a self-sustaining job and an affordable place to live. Those who returned home did so reluctantly, and often with a sense of defeat.

Today, students returning home is a common and accepted next step well into your twenties, and the high number doing so make it possible to go back home without embarrassment. Fewer and fewer parents think their children didn't work hard and weren't willing to make sacrifices as they had.

Don Tapscott, management professor at the University of Toronto, says college grads and older offspring come home willingly. Tapscott interviewed 8,000 young people between the ages of eleven and thirty-one—what he refers to as the Net Generation—all born to baby boomers for his book, *Grown Up Digital*. His findings concur with mine. Many in their twenties said they were happy to move back home. One reason is that boomer offspring and parents grew up in households

---

What Your Parent May Be Thinking

"I want my son to go off on his own, but when he grad-uated, I wasn't really ready for him to move to another state. By having him live with us, I'm buying some more time. I know that this will not be a permanent thing; our time together as a family is limited to a year or two. I see it as a gift."

Donna, fifty-one, mother of a recent college graduate and two younger children.

---

with more give-and-take than did boomers and their parents. Parents and their now-adult children are both ready to live together "democratically," an approach that greatly aids the transition back to family.

People are divided on whether returning home after college is an opportunity to take your time planning what you want to do, to pay off loans and get your financial feet on the

---

What Your Adult Child May Be Thinking

"Friends are critical of my living at home, but I have a chance to construct a future narrative, enact it, and not take some crappy job that I will hate for the rest of my life just to get away from my parents. I have the time and their support to figure out who I am, what I want, what my passion is—a luxury most people don't have."

Hank is a twenty-four-year-old who moved home after graduating from college.

---

ground by saving. This view is counter to one held by those who believe parents are indulging their already overindulged offspring further by protecting them from the real world. While the debate roars on, the reality is that few graduates have a wide field from which to choose. Entry-level jobs are scarce, pay is low, rents are high, and most young graduates just can't make it on their own.

TWENTY-SOMETHINGS RETURN TO THE NEST

Hank is one of many recent college grads who understands and values the benefits of living at home. Andrew Sum, director of the Center for Labor Market Studies at Northeastern University in Boston, says that graduates who accept jobs below their education levels need seven to nine years before their salaries are comparable to the earnings of graduates who take jobs that require a college degree. Yale University School of Management labor economist Lisa Kahn concurs, but thinks that those who accept jobs during a recession can spend longer—up to fifteen years—in the labor force before their earnings catch up with those with comparable educations who start out in better economic times.

Hank is off to graduate school on a scholarship and will avoid a "crappy job," but he's one of the lucky ones. He's getting full freight for advanced education, but others graduate from college, graduate schools, and professional schools with huge debts; $150,000 to $200,000 is not unheard of. *Forbes* magazine reports that the average college student graduates owing $20,000.

To repay education loans, to look for jobs in a tight job market, and to eliminate rents that twenty-somethings can't afford or that would strap them, college grads and older young adults make home their residence of choice. "In these financial times, rather than struggling, it's okay to ask for your parents' help," Chloe, twenty-eight, realized. "I was worried about what my friends would think, but I'm not going to live beyond my means."

Once ensconced, many say, "Why in the world would I want to leave?" As a parent, you may have thought your young adult's arrival home was a stopover, a year, tops, until she found another job or finished her education. Wake-up call: Your college graduate is far too content to think about leaving. Twenty-five-year-old Amanda, who works in hospital administration, feels that she has no reason to leave until she can buy a home of her own. She projects she will live with her parents for another two years. Anyone willing to bet on this one?

Create an Exit Plan Early

Early on, talk about and establish an exit plan with your twenty-something—not a hard-and-fast deadline, but a time frame you all agree on, and within which you expect your child to leave. With a hoped-for plan in place, your son or daughter has a goal to work toward. Without it, you run the risk of enabling and allowing him to coast along and take advantage of the good things you

With a hoped-for plan in place, your son or daughter has a goal to work toward.

provide. A stated date will urge your child toward career success and independence.

Without a solid reason for moving in and a long-range goal for moving out, young adults take a chance when relying on their parents too heavily and losing the sense of purpose necessary to grow as adults. Nina, who returned home after college, grins sheepishly when she says, "I could have stayed forever. I was that comfortable, but I was driven and had mapped out where I wanted to be, and by when."

The Care and Feeding of Prodigal Offspring

If you are a parent, flash back a few years to when your child left home for school or a first apartment, an exit you believed would be permanent. You had gotten through the difficult years and felt a sense of relief; you were more than ready for him to go off, even though your feelings included sadness that he was grown up. Many parents report not being sad at all, recognizing that the family needed the separation.

Elaine recounts her trip to take her daughter to college: "After a stretch of silence, Alexia asked, 'Mom, do you feel sad?' 'No, I don't think so,' I answered, and she came right back with, 'No, neither do I.' It was time, and we both knew it."

Other parents are devastated, not knowing how to fill their days or get rid of that strange feeling in the pit of their stomach. Your empty nest felt, well, empty at first, but after a while, it felt okay, even good. The house stayed shipshape and you didn't have to worry about having meals ready at a preordained hour. You could meet friends and chat on through your usual dinner prep time. You expected your offspring to be mostly independent, and you were free to devote more time to your career, or to start one, to spend extended time with a spouse or take fun trips—bonuses well earned. Once adjusted to life without your son or daughter, his or her return could be a jolt. And, if you prize self-reliance, you could find the return of your grown child a disappointment.

Those who subscribe to "helicopter parenting" feel very differently when their college grads return to the nest. The husband or wife who hasn't cut the cord is happy to have his companion or confidant back in the nest. Labeled "helicopter parents," because they were (and are) in constant contact with their children, they represent an entire generation of parents. Hovering parents worked hard at being their children's best friends, never fully letting go of their mothering-fathering roles.

The husband or wife who hasn't cut the cord is happy to have his companion or confidant back in the nest.

Hara Estroff Marano, editor at large for *Psychology Today* magazine, calls the phenomenon of returning home after college, "perma-parenting." More than ever, parents have become their adult children's fallback position—for longer and longer periods of time. It's comforting to have youth back in the house to stave off parents' feeling of aging, and to be able to continue the closeness. As much as anything else, parents' dependence can prevent an adult child from ever leaving once he or she settles in.

On their end, many twenty-somethings who were raised by helicopter parents pick up right where they left off. "I have no issue checking in with my parents. Communication is constant whether I'm under their roof or not. It's not always them calling me," admits Melissa, twenty-six, who lived with her family after graduate school and returned home again a few months ago because the company she worked for shut its doors. Melissa is hardly alone in her attachment to her parents.

The Pew Research Center found that eight out of ten members of Generation Next, as they call eighteen- to twenty-five-year-olds, spoke to their parents within the last twenty-four hours. Three-fourths of the generation surveyed says that their regular contact is because parents provided money to help them out within the past year.

In spite of the closeness, twenty-somethings who lived away from home as students and as young adults, setting their own schedules and moving at their own pace, don't want parents telling them what to do, in spite of the fact that the same Pew Research discovered that "more than nine in ten are satisfied with their family life (93 percent) and their relationships with their parents (91 percent)." These are outlooks you don't want to tamper with.

You Were Commander in Chief

Your "child" is back for food and shelter, and, sometimes, your ear. The difference between a high school student and college graduate is that the former asks more often. Older young adults tell you what they are doing, and that change of attitude can add to a parent's layers of worry. Jarring and disconcerting to some parents, but as one mother aptly puts it for so many others, "You don't give away your children and/or your pets." You don't, but you do have to talk gingerly about arrangements. If you come on too strong, brace yourself for the "You didn't know what I was doing for the last four years, so why do you have to know now?" or confrontational comments like "It doesn't have to be done this minute, Mom."

Anticipate changes in the person you raised, in your relationship, and in how your household functions, because a returning adult child is not the same one who left a few years ago. He may *Anticipate changes in* have become a political activist, an *the person you raised,* exercise fiend, or a classical music *in your relationship,* buff—all news to you. You see *and in how your* signs of maturity and responsibil- *household functions.* ity that weren't there before, but you also see some of the same-old, same-old behavior.

For the times the parent in you comes out, and you can't stop yourself from butting in, instead of barking orders and making demands, simply say, "I need to tell you this because I'm your parent—you can listen or not. I won't feel like a good parent if I don't speak up." Your "new" boarder is not a guest, but a family member who should share the burden of running the household.

When kids come home there will always be dishes in the sink, or left where they were last used. No longer the helpless toddler and perfectly capable of pitching in, still, it's more than likely you'll have to ask for what you want and be firm about what is unacceptable. We have been living in a culture of yes-parents. Saying *no* is a learned skill, especially when you have to direct it at a child of any age. But if you want to safeguard your time, avoid becoming resentful, and keep peace (and at times your sanity), brush up on your "no" skills, and make optimal use of the word with your boomerang child. For example, say "no" to songs you'll never listen to downloaded onto your computer, or "no" to any other little things that annoy you. Ask your able resident to do some of your laundry, or at least agree that he will take care of his own.

How you say no or make requests is as precarious as deciding what's worth getting worked up about. It's so tempting when you have your grown child home again to call out marching orders: Wear a jacket. Don't forget your lunch. Did you remember to call? The days of being the boss and saying "Take out the garbage," "Run to the store," "Clean up your room," and "Be home by midnight" are essentially over.

As a parent of youngsters, you were commander in chief, or at least acted like it by making pronouncements many times a day. A grown child's return marks the end of order-giving and order-taking as you knew it. Turn in your uniform and megaphone as you navigate the uncharted waters of living with your twenty-something. A certain amount of backing off and holding your tongue is in order.

A grown child's return marks the end of order-giving and order-taking as you knew it.

When you don't, the relationship can deteriorate—sometimes irreparably, as Heather, twenty-four, who has lived at home for the past two years, can attest to: "I thought that the older I got, the more my mother and I would be friends because she didn't have to raise me anymore. But we fight more and she's very nasty. She's constantly telling me to do this or that, followed by "How many times do I have to ask you or tell you." I ask her to stop yelling but that makes her angrier. For me with my mother, it's a lose-lose proposition.

"She doesn't like any of my decisions, from my hairstyle to what I wear—things that are not really her business. We fight so much that I spend most of my time at my boyfriend's. I'm home as little as possible. I don't want to live there anymore. Maybe she'll like me better when I move out and just visit occasionally—if I do."

Unlike Heather's mother, Donna adopts a reflective approach to having her son back home. "I'm putting the same amount of thought into parenting that I did when he was a baby. I try to balance what's best for him, my other children, and for my husband and me." To that end, she holds back in an effort to preserve the good relationship she has with her recent college graduate. She purposefully doesn't appear before he goes to work in the morning so he doesn't feel as if he's back in high school, and she's stopped waking him up in the morning even as she looks at the clock and wonders why she doesn't hear the shower water running. "My husband and I don't harp on the rules, hoping he will rise to the occasion, but mainly because we don't want to make home a battleground and have a break in our relationship that will be hard to repair."

This is your chance to form an adult relationship with the offspring whose baby tears you dried and skinned knees you bandaged. Know when to argue and when to drop the subject. Most of the things you want to discuss are obvious, like cleanliness and noise. Review the Ground Rules on pages 23 to 29 in chapter 2 to learn how you can resolve the basics. And, if there are younger siblings in the home, remind your young adult that his sisters and brothers look up to him; they are watching and learning from him.

OLDER, BUT NOT TOTALLY WISE

It is not easy for a parent to stand by and witness what you believe to be errors in judgment that could be prevented. But, parental suggestions and prodding are not always welcomed by adult children—until they are in trouble.

"My son has an income he can live on, but his poor handling of money is what landed him back on our doorstep," Gordon says of his twenty-six-year-old. "He's way too generous, buys beers for the guys and extravagant gifts for the girlfriend. Like most young people he lives paycheck to paycheck, with no thought of saving for emergencies. He doesn't keep track of what he spends. When he ran out of money and had to come home, I took the opportunity to teach him how to budget so he would have enough money to make his car and insurance payments. I don't object to helping him out, but for all his maturity in other aspects of his life, he didn't have a handle on money. I see he's starting to save . . . finally."

The Associated Press and MTV conducted a study on young people and happiness. The findings, surprisingly, reflect that a parent's advice is very likely to be implemented. Almost half of those asked thought of "at least one of their parents as a hero." Knowing this, you'll want to tell your young adult that you are available to talk if she's concerned about financial obligations, a fallout with a friend, a sizable purchase, going back to school, or a job issue.

THE JOB HUNT

Older single adult children out of school several years, like current college graduates, pound the employment pavement using their parents' homes as a search base. During their job search, it's important to comment with care so you don't inadvertently demean your child, who is working hard to get his life together in a world that's not easy to negotiate. Many graduates are taking jobs in fields they didn't study or that don't necessarily require a college education to pay down their loans, or to contribute to running their parents' households. Young adults, who wonder where their lives are going, need gentle understanding. Without his or her saying it, not knowing what's next in life may be painful for your child, and coming on like a tractor-trailer speeding down the highway will be more irritating than useful.

Not knowing what's next in life may be painful for your child.

You can be an enormous help in putting a floundering child on a better course, but only if you proceed with caution and listen carefully for her ideas on which you can build. Direct questioning—"What you do think you will do?"—is rarely productive, because most college graduates and young adults often don't have an answer. Try not to dwell on the uncertainty, but rather help your son or daughter look at the big picture that will be his life. To the vacillating offspring seemingly without clear direction, you might ask: "What do you feel passionate about? Where do you think you want to be in four or five years?" and then, "Let's try to make a plan to get you there."

An open, relaxed dialogue could lead your young adult into an area not previously considered. As you offer thoughts about jobs or fields of interest, don't force the issue. "I couldn't push it because of my son's temperament," Suzanne says. "I shut my mouth after he left his job and waited for him to bring up his next step. When he said, 'I don't know what I want to do; I didn't like being stuck in an office cubicle all day,' I brought up things he likes—his hobbies. He's very outdoorsy. That led to his going back to school to study landscape architecture. Really, I didn't say much—just tossed out a possibility or two."

Only a few lucky ones with diploma in hand land the job they are going to be in for the next thirty years. You will discover more if you keep a low profile and encourage novice job seekers to gain experience and learn about the working world as they hunt for where they want to be long-term.

How you parented may come into play again as your college grad or older adult child seeks to be gainfully employed. If you are a helicopter parent who called professors to complain about test grades or the dean of housing to register concern about your student's roommate, it's time to stop running interference. The fear, merited or not, that your adult child will never get his or her life together does not justify your swooping in at the slightest chance.

It's time to stop running interference.

True, there are sound reasons for parents to worry about their children's future: Jobs are hard to come by. The National

Association of Colleges and Employers compared 2008 and 2009 employer hiring of college graduates and reported a drop of 22 percent in hiring for entry-level positions. Of the firms surveyed, 17 percent said they would trim college hiring even more in the fall of 2009. In addition, people reaching retirement age are holding on to their jobs; others, to stay afloat, snatch up jobs for which they are overqualified and that would routinely go to recent college grads, further shrinking the opportunity pool for recent college grads. No wonder after seven months of being unemployed, Melissa said, "When I finally landed a job, I felt as if I'd won the lottery."

Carolyn, job recruiter for a major corporation that hires college graduates, is appalled by the amount of parental interference. She admonishes parents who call her with questions about their job applicant. "They leave voicemail messages, sometimes as many as four, telling me to call them back, or letting me know that his son or daughter wants the job. If I do call back, I leave my own message: 'Have your daughter call me.'

"At job fairs it's the mother or father who asks all the questions. That's a dangerous path. Parents should be pushing their children to be in charge. From what I've seen as a recruiter, for many recent college grads who live at home, the scare factor is missing. On the whole, they don't seem worried about being jobless. The attitude is more in the direction of 'If I don't get this job, I can find my dream job. My parents will back me up.' "

To decrease pressure created by the competitiveness and parental over-involvement, assure your young adult that you will always love him, whatever job he takes or how far he succeeds . . . or doesn't.

GIVING OWNERSHIP OF THE JOB HUNT
TO TWENTY-SOMETHINGS

- Remember, it's your son or daughter's job search, not yours.
- Don't do the legwork for your job seeker.
- Offer to *help* create an action plan, with long-term goals.
- Be available to look over the résumé, if asked.
- Provide tips, being sure to qualify them with "I have a thought," or "I heard . . ." or "You might want to check it out."
- Watch for signs that your ideas are being ignored. If you see them, pull back for a month or two and then try again.

THE CARE AND FEEDING OF PARENTS

You might have a parent who is so fearful for her children's futures that she says nothing, or one who doesn't stop nagging. To head off parental worry or harassing on the job front, make finding one a full-time effort. Keep parents up-to-date on your progress so they will worry less. You might consider looking into different opportunities within a field that attracts you. For instance, if you love the film industry and ultimately want to be a director, explore the possibility of editing, writing scripts, or working in menial positions on a film set. Try your hand at a documentary with borrowed equipment and friends as crew if you need assistance. Play any angle you can think of, because most often, determination wins out.

Be prepared for some tension beyond the job search. Your desire to be an independent adult will collide with the inevitability of your parents making you feel incompetent. They may even promise to treat you like a grown-up most of the time, but the propensity to take over your life again is in their blood. In other words, your parents may not have changed all that much during the years you were away.

Grousing came with the territory when you were young. If you had a dime for every time your parents asked you to help with the dishes, mow the lawn, clean up your room, manage your time or money better, or get off the couch, you would be able to afford to rent—or buy—a place of your own. But you don't, and you will be living with them for what will be a goodly amount of time. Because you are living at home, you will have to answer to your parents to some degree, and that is worrisome for many twenty-somethings. They question how they will be able to live under protective parental eyes again.

Testing the Waters

The transition back home with its bumps and minor glitches is easier than you might imagine. You've been home for summers and know pretty much what to expect. Nonetheless, you'll test your parents and they will test you. You may experiment with doing as little to help as possible, or sit glued to your computer, knowing those habits irk your parents. But, as Jeffrey, twenty-six, confirms, "The switch was easy—easier than I thought."

"Having been away, you forget each other's idiosyncrasies," notes Rebecca, who moved home after college. "We all had to readjust and knew that it might take time. Patience is important. You can't be complacent, and you have to be willing to compromise."

Part of compromising means muscling through the sometimes profound dynamics that occur between you and your parents when they make you feel as if you're a teenager again. To keep parents from dealing with you like a child, monitor your own behavior by extending common courtesies, such as calling in if you will be late. As an adult, whether or not you have a job, you are accountable on the home front and expected to act that way.

Watch out for the tendency to revert back to adolescent habits of sloppiness, sulking, or acting out. As Nina, who moved home after college and again after a year in her own apartment, warns, "It's so easy to slip back. I was neat and anal about my things in my apartment. When I moved home, my stuff was everywhere again."

Changing Your Image

Forgetful, sloppy, unreliable, self-centered, uncaring. Could be you were one or all of those things as a child. You have come a long way from having to be reminded to turn out the lights, call your grandmother, or lock the doors. You're not the child who needed constant direction.

The problem is, your parents may still see you as that difficult teenager, and once back in the same house, you may have to prove how different you are. They love you, but their image of the scuffles you all had lingers. When you are one step ahead of them, whatever you tackle will get noticed, and will go a long way toward changing dated perceptions they may be hanging on to.

Reinforcing that the "new you" has replaced the former you banishes negative holdovers. Asking for your parents' advice will earn you a lot of "points" with them, too. To look good in your parents' eyes, you might try to:

- Pitch in more.

- Complete a chore without having to be asked.

- Clean up after yourself.

- Fill the car's gas tank when you use it.

- Alert one of your parents that the other parent's birthday is coming up.

- Tell a parent to relax and take it easy—you'll water the flowers or lawn for them.

- Bring your mother flowers for no reason.

- Take the initiative in your free time to repair a broken railing, tighten a screw, or offer to paint a room that could use sprucing up.

THE ULTIMATE PLUS FOR EVERYONE

When friends are fleeing the nest, some young adults put a lot of pressure on themselves to move out because they "feel emasculated" still living with their parents, according to Hank.

Not Andrew, who moved back home at twenty-five. He and twenty-somethings like him are not leaving anytime soon. Before he returned home, he had a wonderful apartment that he could afford on his salary, until he quit his job. He went back to stay in his old bedroom where he's been for the last four years. Recently his mother told him about a friend who had just moved out of his parents' home into his own apartment, to which Andrew remarked, "Been there, did that—overrated."

His mother chimes in, "After four years at home with me, Andrew alludes to having an apartment one day, but I cook at least three times a week, pay the rent, and interfere in his life as little as possible. That all makes hanging around here preferential to anything he might do on his own right now."

As an adult child, you will want to be cognizant of the very real advantages you have—food, shelter, and time to determine where you want to go so you don't end up in a job you dislike for much longer than you thought you would be there. And, parents will want to avoid making life at home so comfortable that their adult children see no need to leave. Pay attention to the timelines you've set—or will set—and revisit them occasionally so you don't wind up with a forty- or fifty-year-old who has never left the nest.

"I had to live away from my parents before I could appreciate them and the time we had together when I moved back," recalls Eric, who plans to return home for the third time as an adult. "We now engage each other as friends because I'm older. I like spending time with my parents. We talk about ideas and interests, and that is so much more pleasant than the relationship of parent and teenager."

TO MAKE TIME TOGETHER CONGENIAL
- Respect those you live with.
- Be sensitive to the problems faced by your "housemates."
- Make suggestions, not pronouncements.
- Observe common courtesies with all family members.
- Understand that living together is a give-and-take proposition.
- Keep conversations away from sensitive, hot-button subjects.
- Decide what's important to press for and what to let go.
- Be appreciative of the time you have together.

There's little doubt that the relationship between adult child and parents has to be tweaked as parents and twenty-somethings join forces again. The by-product of living together is the ability to gain an understanding of each other as adults, as people rather than just as parent and child. For that reason alone, assure your son or daughter that you will always be there to provide a roof over his or her head, unless you feel as time goes on that your grown child is "using" you and not getting on with his life.

Chapter Ten

Older and Headed Home

You may have recently bragged about your daughter's last promotion, stood proudly at the altar witnessing your son's marriage, or shared the elation of the birth of your grandchildren—or their graduations. These are all milestones that parents celebrate, and that signify their adult children are independent. Often, and without much warning, parents are called on again to provide a safe haven from whatever obstacle has been thrown in their adult child's path.

Older adult children are just as likely as twenty-somethings to ask the "Can I come home?" question. They, too, can arrive for reasons that range from dismal circumstances to pure convenience. In spite of the difficulties you all may face in resolving the problems that bring adult children home, their return presents an opportunity to form a new kind of personal relationship. When you enjoy being together, you build a warm, close, peer-to-peer relationship and set in motion the beginnings of a true friendship that will last a lifetime.

In your thirties, forties, fifties (and older), uprooting to go home can be extremely disruptive, whether you're moving back voluntarily or because of a personal crisis. Planned and unplanned shifts in residences can be hard on everyone. In some cases, parents worry that they represent too much of a protective shield against the real world, while at the same time, they wouldn't dream of turning their offspring away.

What Your Parent May Be Thinking

"My daughter is back for a return engagement. Last time she came home for two years, but stayed ten. I don't see this stay ending anytime soon. What can I do? I can't put them on the street."

Elizabeth's daughter, fifty, arrived six months ago with her husband and Elizabeth's twenty-something grandchild.

READY OR NOT, HERE I COME

No parent wants to see a child of any age in bad straits and miserable. Parents rarely abandon their adult children when businesses go bust, jobs get lost, mortgages can't be met, houses can't be sold, or relationships crumble. In a fragile state of mind, both parents and adult child can feel as if so much has been lost or given up. The adult child may not be able to picture what he'll be doing next month.

Going home at any age may be the one sure thing at that moment in an adult child's life. In many situations, there is no

---

What Your Adult Child May Be Thinking

"My parents understand me. Growing up they gave me lots of freedom. At twenty-three, I could come home at 4:00 a.m. without hearing about it. I know it will be okay to live there with my girlfriend until she and I decide where we want to be."

Jeremy, thirty-three, lived at home in one- and two-year chunks since graduating college.

---

better sanctuary when your life becomes unsettled. A nasty breakup could have an adult child headed home with no warning. You discover the person you planned to marry is cheating. Or, you didn't see your marriage falling apart, or foresee that the company you have been loyal to for years would decide to purge whole divisions, including yours. Your parents don't expect you, but there you are on their doorstep: miserable, computer tucked safely on the car floor, clothing in hand, and maybe a few children nestled behind you.

For Kristen, thirty-one, the marital bickering had escalated to an unbearable point. "I didn't call my parents. I just got in my car one day with my cat and my stuff and drove seven hours to their house. I had no plan. I knew I'd hear a lot about my husband's keeping all our money and my parents wanting me to be okay. They don't think I can do anything on my own. I knew it wasn't going to be easy."

At times, you may feel overprotected or get on each other's nerves, especially if space is in short supply. It can also feel odd to live with your furniture in storage or to have to listen to someone else tediously recount her day when you're used to being alone. So much to adapt to: finances to juggle, schedules to adjust, physical living space to alter, cars to share, and, perhaps, someone's food preferences to take into consideration. As you've read, these adjustments can be accomplished successfully at most any age when flexibility and understanding take center stage.

Life stressors unrelated to living together may make someone in the house short-tempered or irritable. And, alcoholism and drug use are difficult to live with under any circumstances.

Nicole's reasons for living with her parents were part choice, part need. She and her husband are committed to her being a stay-at-home mom. They can't afford to live on one salary, at least not until her husband gets a promotion or a better-paying job. Initially, they lived with Nicole's parents, until her father's drinking made it impossible for them to stay. They moved in with her in-laws. "I didn't want my children seeing my father's unpredictable drinking behavior. My in-laws create such a positive environment. They play with my eighteen-month-old and teach him things continuously. He gets so much healthy attention."

When the impetus to move home is a divorce or separation, neither parents nor offspring may have time to think about how or if the arrangement will be amenable. "I was in emotional shambles from the end of a relationship with the man I lived with and thought I was marrying," says Jessica, thirty-two. "I was thinking about me, not about how living with my parents would pan out. We didn't talk about any arrangements. My paying rent has become the central argument. My parents blame me for the money I invested in a house that I can't sell in this market. They keep repeating that if I weren't in such a financial hole, I could be paying them rent—as if I didn't know that."

BEYOND THE BLAME GAME

By the time adult children reach their thirties and forties, parents blaming them for poor decisions should be a thing of the past. Adult children come home for understanding and support, not to be told what they should have done or what they should be doing. Unlike the recent college grad or younger adult who is finding her way, if a parent attempts to micromanage your life, you need to express your discomfort. This is your parent's problem, not yours. You have led an independent life and know you have to face the residual difficulties that your decisions or your life's circumstances may have spawned.

You Might Say:

- "I got myself in this mess, I'll get myself out."

- "I love that you want to help me, but I need to work on this myself."

- "Let me try. I will ask for your advice if I need it."

- "I will feel so much better about myself if I take charge."

- "At this stage of my life, I need to stand on my own two feet."

In a *New York Times* article about his writing and life, novelist Colm Toibin points out the reverse position: "I think arriving home and accusing your mother of things when you're in your 30s and she's in her 60s or 70s is not something you should do. People are getting older, they have enough on their minds without their children arriving in states of hysteria or accusation."

When you see your parent every day, you may wonder why your father doesn't watch his weight or why your mother buys more dresses than she could possibly wear. Your parent may be hooked on what you consider "junk" television and you want to enlighten him. He may put on the same tattered sweater every morning and you wish he would wear the new one you just gave him. It's not your job to fix the things that perplex you. In the interest of harmony, ignore, don't attack; don't try to correct your parents' personal failings or oddities as you see them. Parents are entitled to their predilections.

WHEN PARENTS DISAGREE

If an adult child plans to hunker down in your home with a husband and a child or two of her own, friends may be astonished when it sinks in that you are quite excited. After the call from her daughter asking to move back with her husband and children, Ruth proclaimed, "I couldn't wait for them to arrive. I was thrilled." Not every parent is overjoyed.

Parents who were on the same page the entire time they were raising their children often veer in different directions when an adult child returns, and stays. You may be pushing your child out or encouraging independence at the same time your spouse is not ready for the separation. Over the last ten years Francine's husband Jack periodically objects to his daughter, son-in-law, and grandchildren sharing their home. "Jack likes to tell me that I already raised two children and I shouldn't be doing this again. I don't pay attention because I know he really doesn't mean it. He loves those kids."

Donna talked about how much she enjoys the "gift of time" with her twenty-something son; others with older children living at home can come to feel that the gift of time is wearing thin. When stays turn into years and decades, there's likely to be more disagreement about the direction in which an adult child is heading . . . or not heading.

Husband and wife may have been in agreement initially, but as time drags on they come to different conclusions. When George's daughter arrived home at age twenty-four, both parents believed it was the best thing for her; today, she's almost forty and continues to live with her parents. "My wife wants her family around more than anything else. Her children are her security blanket," George says. "It's convenient to have someone in the house if we go away, but our daughter, who once had no direction, is a successful radiologist now. She can afford to rent or buy a place of her own. As much as I enjoy her, it's time for her to move on."

CHOOSING TO LIVE WITH PARENTS

Many returns to live with parents are *not* about a life disappointment, romance gone awry, job loss, or financial struggle. They are voluntary: Older adult children live with their parents because it makes undeniable practical sense, because they want to, or in the back of their minds, they always thought they would.

Many returns to live with parents are not about a life disappointment, romance gone awry, job loss, or financial struggle.

When Ann got divorced, she snapped at the chance to buy her childhood home from her mother who lived in it—a dream she had had for many years. She and her mother have been living together amicably for three years. They've compromised in order to adjust to each other's different styles, but Ann makes her position clear: "Aside from the incredible care I get, I don't have to cook or clean; I raised three kids and am enjoying *not* doing that.

"I love listening to my mother's stories about the old days, which come out in the course of conversation. I will not move again. I didn't feel good about Mother living alone, and am very lucky to still have my mother."

Ann's mother expresses similar sentiments. "It's nice to have company and someone to do things with. I hated cooking just for myself, so I eat better."

Although the circumstances for going home vary, the outcome is the same: a move home with Mom or Dad, or both. Monica's return to the nest was inspired solely by her desire to advance her acting career. At the age of fifty-three, she left the Midwest and her husband to be in New York City, the heart of the nation's theater industry. For the past three years her husband visits for a month at a time while she studies acting and performs whenever she lands a part. She feels living with her parents works because, as she says, "I am a different person than I was as a child. The more assured I became being the adult I had grown to be, the more comfortable the relationship became. I don't use children's language when I speak to my parents. I talk to them as I would to other adults, to my friends."

Some find that if they stop *thinking* of their parents as Mom and Dad, it's easier to make the leap to considering them friends. Others make the switch by calling their parents by their first names, or relating to parents as if they were just getting to know a new friend.

Monica also realizes that as an adult, she can act like one. Instead of arguing about her and her parents' different political perspectives, which could turn volatile, she walks away from those discussions. "If my parents are watching FOX News, I leave the room. It's that simple. I address the immediate situation rather than balking like a child whose desires and wants don't mesh with her parents'."

Knowing you get along and enjoy each other's company is reason enough to return home.

You, too, may long be over the power struggles and arguments you had with your parents, or know how to handle them without hassles. Knowing you get along and enjoy each other's company is reason enough to return home. You might want to be near your family while you realign your life's direction.

Sometimes happenstance moves you toward your family permanently. Linda is sixty and divorced, with two adult children who live in other states. Two years ago Linda moved closer to her parents to help out during her dad's illness. She thought the move would be temporary, but stayed after he died and found a job in the area. Her brother and sister both live nearby, and everyone is pleased that the family is together. She allows that "the jump from thinking this was a temporary move to making it a permanent one was difficult.

"I see the experience as humbling. It's not just me anymore to consider. If Mom or I get sick, we're here for each other. I feel more secure in my relationship with her than I did as a child. Then I was the rebel in the family, and still am, but my mother has become more tolerant of me. She accepts my switch to a different church and my desire to be my own person. If I were dating, she'd be happy for me. She's more than a housemate, because there's a lot more emotion involved. She's more like a friend. Whatever she needs, I'm here for her."

MY PARENT/MY FRIEND

You're living together as adults, not as parents raising children or children being raised. A parent-friend rarely lets you down. He's there to boost you up and is almost always 100 percent on your side.

"I had a close relationship with my dad, and having my son home lets me fulfill my desire to have a close relationship with him," says Gordon, fifty-seven. "We interact every day, and he comes to me with his problems. He'll ask me how I would handle or what do I think about a certain situation. He even discusses his girlfriend difficulties. He knows I will always tell him the truth about anything he asks. Knowing he trusts me and comes to me is very flattering."

It's quite common to hear adult children say, "My parents are my best friends." Many parents of all ages feel that way, too. Dorothy, eighty-six, boasts of her friendship with her fifty-three-year-old daughter: "Everyone predicted having my daughter move in with me would be a disaster because we're completely different. Among other things, she's not neat and I am; I'm very social, and she doesn't do as much as I do. The naysayers were wrong. We get along so well even though we are opposite personalities. I'm her best friend."

As parent–adult child friendships form, it's important to be aware that no single peer friendship satisfies all of a person's needs. Most people have one friend who is a confidant, another with whom they might share a special interest, and yet another who can be counted on to be there in an emergency. We love one friend for her fun personality, but might not share our very personal problems with her. Another friend is great for shopping, but you wouldn't ask her how to get your child to sleep at night. Even our closest friends have limitations in meeting all of our friendship needs.

With parents and adult children, the foundation for friendship is distinct. By being together during the formative years, the relationship automatically includes most of the core elements of rock-solid peer friendship.

THE TEN CORE ELEMENTS OF FRIENDSHIP

1. A shared history
2. Concern and caring
3. Support and trust
4. Mutual respect
5. Love and affection
6. Forgiveness
7. Acceptance
8. Respect of privacy
9. Ability to listen
10. Common interests

As you reinvent the relationship with your parent or adult child, home in on its strengths. Your shared history and concern for each other—hard to match with the oldest or dearest of friends—give you a giant head start. It's unlike any bond you have with a friend if for no other reason than it goes back farther.

Exercising good judgment in what you share will preserve your developing peer-to-peer friendship. In much the same way you would protect a friend, you will want to withhold information that is disturbing or might worry your adult child or parent—the details of an unsavory love relationship, for example.

> *Exercising good judgment in what you share will preserve your developing peer-to-peer friendship.*

Use the time you have together to share mutual interests and to explore new ones. Figure out what might be fun, challenging, or get you both engaged: Buy a Scrabble game, learn a new language, be your own two- or three-person book club, or volunteer for a cause you believe in. Anything you do together will improve how you relate. One mutual interest can be enough to sustain the friendship.

It's never too late to form a friendship with someone in your family. Applying the ten core elements that distinguish good friendships will ease you into one with your son or daughter or parent. And, given that you have a natural starting point and are living together again, there's no excuse not to.

THOUGHTS ON BECOMING LOVING ALLIES

- Respect your differences.
- Don't try to change each other.
- Talk to each other as you would talk to your friends.
- Work toward an equitable collaboration.
- View the friendship as a work in progress.
- Plan things to do together.
- Make time for your adult child or parent.
- There's always room for improvement.

Chapter Eleven

Parents and In-Laws Moving In

As soon as you mention that your mother or father, or, more shocking, your in-laws, are coming to live with you, there is an almost visceral response from those you tell. It's usually far more vehement than when you announce that your adult child is returning. In utter disbelief and with undisguised horror in their voices, they say, "Are you out of your mind?" "How will that work?"

You agreed to have your mother-in-law live with you for three months. Time flies—she's been in your house for thirteen years. It seemed wrong to leave your dad alone after your mother died, so you invited him for a monthlong visit. That was six years ago.

One Texas couple had both fathers in their home at the same time for four years; the husband's dad married and moved away, only to return when his second wife died. To hear Harriet recount their unusual story, there's no question that she and her husband loved every minute of it. "We called them 'the boys,' both widowed, both in their early sixties, and both with the same first name. They acted like siblings, going out together and delighting in tattling on each other. They ate dinner with us or got in the car and went off on their own. They'd come home and play cards into the night.

"My husband and I are both only children. For our children, their grandfathers were their family—no aunts, uncles, or cousins. They saw the value of family being close. At no time were we angry or disappointed, and 'the boys' had such a good time with each other. My father's stay was supposed to be temporary, but he was enjoying himself too much to leave to live alone. I think it was easy because my husband and I talked about the impact on our lives before we suggested a move-in to 'the boys.' "

When joining forces succeeds, the arrangement can be filled with new insights into your parents or your partner's parents. While these living situations are rarely without glitches, they are almost always worth the trade-off. Sarah, a single mother of four, has logged in twelve years living with her parents, seven of them while she was still married. "My parents had nothing to do with causing our divorce," Sarah explains. "As a single parent for the last five years, I appreciate their sharing responsibilities. They help prepare dinner and do much of the chauffeuring detail. We've created a little village in which everyone helps and cares for one another."

"We've created a little village in which everyone helps and cares for one another."

Like Sarah and the Texas couple, many adult children want their parents and divorced or widowed mothers and fathers to live with them. In African American cultures, particularly in the South, multigenerational living is accepted and expected, as it is in many European and Asian cultures. "When I tell people my mother lives with me, they look at me strangely. I always thought that would happen; the reverse never occurred to me," says Sandra, sixty-one, whose mother came to live with her

---

What Your Parent May Be Thinking

"I watched my mother take care of her mother for six-teen years—my grandmother didn't have to lift a fin-ger. When I moved in with my daughter, I thought she would take care of me. It doesn't seem to be working out that way: My daughter expects me to help with my grandchildren and help around the house. She won't back down."

Cynthia, seventy-two, has been living with her daughter's family since her husband died six months ago.

---

after her father's death. "Having my mother living by herself was unnerving for me. Now I know she is safe and loved and with people who love her. Before my father died, I spoke with them three or four times a week, but I only saw my parents once or twice a year because of the distance and expense of travel. I feel at peace with her being here, a peace I didn't feel for the thirty years she was so far away."

What Your Adult Child May Be Thinking

"I'd like more consideration and less control from my mother. She should be asking herself, 'What can I do to make life easier for the people I live with?' Instead, she's trying to run the show. She lives with us and has to realize we have problems, too."

Peter, thirty-eight, moved his mother in to live with him, his wife, and their two young children.

When parents or in-laws move in, it's often thought to be long-term. You may be looking ahead to a time when parents will need more assistance than they do now; perhaps their financial picture is grim and not likely to change; maybe sharing expenses helps you both; or, they (or you) are lonesome—all good reasons for sharing a home. Knowing that it's probably permanent makes it more imperative to be sure everyone understands the reasons and the arrangements.

WE ALL AGREE

Inviting your parents or in-laws to live with you is a decision to make together, and one you want everyone, including your children, to feel good about. Some families "test-drive" living together by having parents or in-laws stay for long weekends, adding on more days each week until they are a constant presence. With Peter's mother, there was no time for a trial period, for easing in. She did not want to live with her son and his family and pointedly made their relationship difficult by butting in and not lifting a finger to help.

To avoid creating an impossible or sticky situation, you'll want to have several serious discussions with those moving in *and* with your partner. Parents or in-laws could well be thinking one thing, while you, or you and your spouse, are thinking another. Discussions have two distinct purposes: one, to prepare parents or in-laws for what you see as meeting immediate needs—theirs or yours—and possible ways to address them, and two, to go over how they visualize day-to-day living and any eventualities.

Robert, forty-two, went to great lengths to comfort his father after his mother died, but didn't plan ahead. A few months before her unexpected death, he had purchased a small one-bedroom home which he decided to rent out so he could help his father get resituated. He and his dad packed up his childhood home and rented a two-bedroom home for them to share. Although Robert thought he and his father would be together for a year, it's already been two. "I don't have a good exit strategy yet," he says. "I don't want to abandon him, but I'd like to go back to my house."

Before the Move: Questions to Ask

- What effect will having parents or in-laws in your house have on your lives?

- Is this arrangement permanent or temporary? Specify time limits if you know you are planning to move, retire and scale back, sell your home, etc.

- What space is available for a parent or in-law?

- Will it affect us financially? In a positive or negative way?

- Does your spouse get along well with your parent(s)?

- How will we handle a parent(s)'s possessions?

- How do our children relate to the grandparent(s) soon to live with us?

- What is the plan if it doesn't work out or someone's relationship status changes?

UNDERSTANDING PARENTS AND IN-LAWS

There's not always time to find the answers to all these questions, or to resolve the points they raise, but there is time to reflect on personalities and the relationship you've had in the past. Such an analysis will help you project how things might turn out. Will you hardly know your parent is in the house? Or will yours be the type you can't get away from?

A difficult parent or in-law will in all likelihood remain a difficult or somewhat difficult parent in the new surroundings you provide. He or she might have mellowed with age, but count on signs of the personality you remember cropping up now and then. An entitled parent may believe that you have children so that they will take care of you; a selfish one will demand the full load of cable programming when he's the only one who watches television on a consistent basis. The frivolous parent will throw two pieces of clothing in the washing machine instead of waiting for everyone's dirty clothes, having no regard for the family's reduced income or electricity costs.

Four years ago Judy started out optimistic about her mother-in-law living with them, but almost immediately, her mother-in-law's self-centered side resurfaced. "She won't join us for dinner when my family is here because she doesn't like my sister; she won't join us when we have friends in; and she's barely civil to her grown-up grandchildren. If anyone is visiting, she goes to her room and won't say hello to people she's known for decades. If she can't be the center of attention, she is antisocial. We invite her less and less and don't feel the least bit guilty about it.

"My husband knows his mother is self-absorbed and he can live with it. I'm not opposed to multigenerational living, but my mother-in-law is just not the right person. If I weren't patient, I would have put her out a long time ago."

Sandra, sixty-one, is sure her mother is the right person. "She's accommodating and neat. She may comment on things I do that disturb her, like my lack of neatness, but she doesn't go in my room or follow me around, picking up what I leave behind. We get along. I made up my mind our living together would be successful, and it is."

LIVING TOGETHER POINTERS
FOR ADULT CHILDREN

- Be respectful of parents and in-laws even when they are challenging.
- Carve out a corner for yourself where you can retreat for some peace and quiet.
- Designate a certain time of day for spending time alone with your spouse and children.
- Don't cart your parents or in-laws everywhere with you, or on every family vacation.
- Be wary of a troublemaking parent who tries to come between husband and wife.
- Let your partner confront his or her parent when problems arise.

Don't Underestimate What a Parent Can Do

Keeping peace and the household purring along require effort on everyone's part. You may want help, or you may choose to do everything yourself. Harriet selected the latter option for "the boys." "They were happy to be taken care of, and I was willing to do it. I think males are easier. You don't have the 'I want to get in the kitchen and/or run the house' issues."

Helpful parents pose their own distinctive problem. Yolanda doesn't like the way her mother cleans up after dinner, but allows her to do it anyway. She waits until her parents go to their room to wipe down the counters and put things in place the way she likes them. That often means staying up later than she normally would. "I don't want to hurt their feelings when I know they are trying to be supportive."

Age and ability are considerations, but being older doesn't mean a parent can't help. He may choose not to, or not know what to do. You could have a parent who is a lot stronger than you are, who can pick up your four-year-old with one arm, or one who can manage your money and hers more effectively than you can. Usually it just takes notification or direction to get the assistance you need. But, if the senior living with you starts out dependent for most things, from shelter to entertainment, or, if like Cynthia's mother, the only model she knows is her mother taking care of her grandmother, a more-proactive approach is called for.

Age and ability are considerations, but being older doesn't mean a parent can't help.

After five decades of marriage and mutual reliance, Dawn's mother moved in with her and her two children. "I think she believed that I was going to care for her like my father did, but I'm a single mother who has to earn a living and support my two children.

"I told my mother that the kids are my top priority. She should understand that I'm single, with no ex sending me monthly checks. I'm not waiting on my mother hand and foot, although sometimes it feels as if I have another child in the house. I wonder who's babysitting whom when one of my children tells me Grandma didn't give them lunch. I know I can't change all her seventy-five-year-old habits overnight, but I can teach her how to be independent and how to help me."

HELPING A PARENT HELP HERSELF . . . AND YOU

- Encourage your parent to make her own phone calls.
- Offer advice on decisions that may be complicated, or that she's never had to make on her own, so she's not taken advantage of.
- Review the tasks that she needs to do each day until they become automatic.
- Spell out instructions clearly, if necessary.
- Do a "dry run" to places she will have to go or take the children so she can get there by herself.
- Let her know that you are glad she could take a chore off your hands whenever she does.

DEALING WITH QUIRKS AND DIFFICULTIES

No matter how committed you are to making living together a positive experience, the smallest details or differences in how another person tackles a task can become a constant barb. Someone's upbringing may account for what appears silly to you, or they may have a different way of doing things that defies your sense of logic. For instance, you may have a parent who is adamant about expiration dates on food products. You go to the refrigerator for milk or cream cheese only to discover that it's been discarded—expiration date yesterday. Your parent or in-law puts food away uncovered or stores household items in places where you can't find them. Or, you own a dishwasher, but your parent is content, actually prefers, to hand-wash dishes from a meal for ten people.

By the time parents are living with their adult children, it's likely that they are somewhat set in their ways. Washing dishes by hand is a habit to ignore. However, you might want to try to alter or amend the quirks that interfere or slow you down by saying: "It bothers me when I can't find the paper towels. Can we agree on where they go so we can both find them?" Or, "I understand how you feel about expiration dates, but instead of throwing things out, please leave them. The rest of us will use them or I'll throw them out when I think they're unsafe." The other option is to adopt the attitude that trivial annoyances are just that—trivial, and not worth getting worked up about.

Some behaviors are hard to overlook. Issues pertaining to safety and health call for establishing strict parameters. One transgression can lead to a huge *Issues pertaining to* confrontation with long-lasting *safety and health call* effects. When a critical rule has *for establishing strict* been broken, it's near impossible *parameters.* not to lose your temper at the transgressor, or to feel like you can trust them again.

Eileen's in-laws were in their seventies and her children were five and eleven years old at the time her in-laws moved in to an addition built just for them; the kitchen was used jointly. During her toddler years, Eileen's daughter had developed a dangerous allergy to shellfish, which her in-laws, of course, were told. They were not permitted to bring any shellfish or premade foods into the house because a shellfish product may have been used in the preparation. "We have only one rule: You can't bring foods into this house that will kill my daughter. It's more than a rule—it's law," Eileen explains.

"My in-laws are Asian and prepare a lot of their own meals, many of which include fish, but they understood the dangers of shellfish from day one, almost ten years ago. They know we keep emergency medication in the house. A few years ago I opened the garbage can and saw shrimp shells; I was beside myself with rage and confronted my mother-in-law. The incident damaged my daughter's relationship with her grandparents, and I don't trust them anymore."

When you got married, the last thing you thought about, if it crossed your mind at all, was that you would be living with both or one of your in-laws. For every impossible in-law, there's a divine one—one you wished were your mother or father. Still, you could feel angry because your mother- or father-in-law is alive and your own parent died years ago. Don't expect your in-law to act like your parent would.

You could be faced with an in-law who believes no one is good enough for her son or daughter. She's apt to question or challenge your every move, and tell *you* and your friends about it. Jacqui is into her twenty-second year of sharing her home with her mother-in-law. "When my friends propose nominating me for sainthood, I nod my head in agreement and say, 'I accept.' Her outrageousness has kept me on my toes."

Jacqui tackles her in-law wisely by having her husband talk to his mother in an attempt to stop her constant criticism and fairy tales. "My mother-in-law is nonstop critical of me to *my* family, who loyally report back to me. She could have affected our marriage if we'd let her, but we had a nine-year solid base before she moved in. My husband always sticks up for me, takes my side, and handles the difficulties with his mother."

Having grown up with a parent, the son or daughter knows his parent far better than you do, and will be able to pick the best time and approach for handling a problem. When you ask a spouse to speak for you, you can also argue that you want to keep your relationship with your in-law on an even keel, or that your in-law will accept correction or information better from her own child.

If you have a partner who is very protective of his or her parent and not supportive of you, find someone else to vent to. Friends or relatives with in-laws (or parents) in their home will be happy to listen to your major and minor grievances and commiserate. Ornery in-law behavior becomes less so when you crank up your sense of humor and share your trials with someone in the same position. Developing the ability to tune out an in-law's antics is useful, too.

SMART DECISIONS FOR THE ENTIRE FAMILY

Discussion is the grown-up way to handle differences and frustrations. When something isn't working out as you or a parent thought it would, one of you should broach the subject. Contend with it sooner rather than later so the annoyance doesn't have time to fester. Consider creating a family house rule: If anyone is unhappy about something going on in this house, speak up so we can try to fix it or change it. Ask for ideas that will improve or eliminate the problem. For changes to work, everyone has to bend, if only because there are more people in the house to please.

When something isn't working out as you or a parent thought it would, one of you should broach the subject.

When parents and in-laws arrive, certain aspects of your life become more complicated; others become easier. Your attention will be divided, as will your time. However, the parents or in-laws who live with you can be sous chefs or head chefs, or full-time groundskeepers. In whatever role they serve, they are, more often than not, loyal supporters of the family, even if you can't bring yourself to call your mother-in-law "Mom."

As challenges arise, think back to the times your parents or in-laws were less problematic. Talk about the good memories, and change the subject if it veers in an unhappy or argumentative direction. Ask about your own or your spouse's childhood, or point the conversation in the direction of your children's activities or accomplishments. This approach will help to keep exchanges on an affable course.

TIP SHEET FOR PARENTS AND IN-LAWS

- Follow any existing "house rules," or request a change if a rule doesn't work for you.
- Consider the pressures your adult children face.
- Think about what might be helpful, but don't take over.
- Tempting as it may be, don't reorganize the kitchen or straighten adult children's dresser drawers.
- Refrain from being meddlesome or cranky.
- Instead of complaining, ask about fixing a problem.
- Have your own social life so you are not completely dependent on your adult children.

MODELING FOR THE NEXT GENERATION

If you have young children or teenagers living at home, don't overburden them with too much responsibility for their grandparents. Have them assist grandparents within reason if they need it. Most important is for adult children and parents or in-laws to be as close and supportive of each other as possible.

Your children are watching the fun you have together, the respect you show, and the care you give. In other words, you are modeling for your children. How you treat and interact with your parents or in-laws is the way your children will probably relate to you in the future.

Sarah looks at the long-range benefit for her children. "It was very important for my parents to retire near one of their children so that they could be part of their grandchildren's lives. My children are experiencing the challenges of three generations in one household, and that in itself is teaching them about honoring boundaries and being easygoing. They are learning to be more sensitive to others and gaining an emotional depth that many of their friends won't have."

ROLE MODEL GUIDE

- Monitor what you say.
- Keep the relationship convivial.
- Be patient.
- Be thoughtful and kind.
- Don't be afraid to show emotion and affection.
- Remember—your children and grandchildren are observing.

Chapter Twelve

"Grandma Said I Could"

JUST ABOUT THE TIME PARENTS ARE GETTING OLDER AND BELIEVING their parenting days are over, they are back in the thick of it— this time helping to care for their grandchildren. Almost everyone agrees that the bond between parents and adult children is enhanced when grandchildren arrive. However, when grandparents live with their offspring and grandchildren, a different approach to "parenting" is called for. There's a shift in power, and parenting ideally becomes a cooperative effort, with adult children in the leading role. Grandparents must accept and respect the new hierarchy.

There's a shift in power, and parenting ideally becomes a cooperative effort.

In spite of the changed order, grandparents remain the force that keeps family connected. They hold the family history; they pass on traditions; and they are the principal cheerleaders for both adult children and grandchildren. The potential rewards of close parent-child and grandparent-grandchild relationships increase when you all live together. Visits with grandchildren are wonderful, but sharing meals, bedtime rituals, and a good story or joke on a daily basis lets a grandparent understand how a grandchild thinks and what makes her so special.

If you're contemplating having a grandparent or two live with you, or you and your children are moving in with Grandma and Grandpa, it's reassuring to know that in the majority of cases, the arrangement helps everyone. Julia, fifty-one, thinks "having my mother live with us teaches my children that they can do things for other people. Her presence keeps them from being selfish and makes them more responsible. There's another person in the house that they have to consider."

Living together is an opportunity to form lasting bonds with grandchildren. Every single day, live-in grandparents can encourage grandchildren's pursuits and cheer them on—or cheer them up—when their parents are unavailable. Today's health-conscious seniors are far more likely than earlier generations of grandparents to stay in shape and have the energy to chase a two-year-old, teach a five-year-old to ride a bike, or shoot baskets with a teenager. You may have to tell a grandparent to take it easy, but he probably won't.

THE "FIRST GRANDMA" SETS THE STAGE

As more and more grandparents assume full-time and part-time care for their grandchildren, it's clear that they can be a parent's lifesaver. Where would the Obamas be without Michelle Obama's mother? Marian Robinson watched her grandchildren while Barack and Michelle Obama campaigned, and she watches over them while her daughter and son-in-law travel extensively, both in and out of the country. The Obama administration's First Grandma has set the stage, unleashing a flurry of interest in grandparents helping adult children raise their children and cope with job demands and financial problems.

What Your Parent May Thinking

"I have a friend whose grandchildren live in England and she rarely gets to see them. She reminds me how lucky I am to have my grandchildren living with me. It's amazing to watch them grow, but my patience is not what it used to be."

Francine is fifty-four. Her three grandchildren, ages ten, seven, and three, have lived with her since they were born.

It wasn't always the case that a grandparent in the White House was the answer to the demands of the President and First Lady's public life and their resulting insane schedules. Franklin Roosevelt's mother, Sara Delano Roosevelt, made life difficult for Eleanor with her strong will and opinions. Sara advised Eleanor in the rearing of her children and dominated family life. Eleanor Roosevelt realized that her mother-in-law's

---

What Your Adult Child May Be Thinking

"On the downside, my parents always put in their two cents. It's not convenient to hear something you don't want to hear at that moment. My mother tells my children what to do, repeatedly reminding them of chores, or to study more so people will think they're smart. In having an opinion on everything, my parents give my four kids someone else to be mad at and not just at me."

Sarah, forty-eight and a divorced mother of four, has lived with both of her parents for twelve years.

---

loyalty to family was her most admirable trait, but by most accounts, it was loyalty taken too far.

Your living conditions probably won't be as glorious as those in the White House—bedrooms will be smaller—and grandparents won't have all the help they need. Still, the presence of a grandparent offers stability that only a family member can provide. In that and most other respects, the First Grandma is not very different from the millions of grandparents who move in to assist their adult children and sons- and daughters-in-law.

"Family-friendly" was to be the overriding "rule" for those who work with President Obama, but as Peter Orszag, a member of Obama's staff, told the *New York Times*, Orszag often "imports his parents to help care for his nine-year-old daughter and seven-year-old son."

Your reasons for living as a multigenerational family may be different from those with high-power White House jobs, but the principles required to keep immediate family relationships loving are the same. Having a grandparent live with you reduces or eliminates child-care costs, and allows parents to go to work with far fewer concerns than they might have with "hired" help.

After many attempts to find suitable child care for her daughter, Hannah, forty-four, and her husband decided to try his mother as the live-in caregiver for their baby. "She was amazingly competent. She catered to my daughter from the time she was seven months old through high school," says Hannah. "Giving in to her every whim was counter to what I intended, but it was a trade-off worth making. I got to go to work, worry-free."

As parents work longer hours, live-in grandparents provide relief for their harried adult children. Grandparents sit on the sidelines at soccer games,

Live-in grandparents provide relief for their harried adult children.

take children to doctor appointments, nurse children's colds, and attend recitals when parents cannot. It is reassuring and priceless for parents to know that the people looking after their children are as devoted to them as they are.

GENERATING TRUST

Caring for grandchildren can be frustrating at times, for both parents and grandparents, but wise parents and grandparents make the situation manageable for everyone by building trust and recognizing that the children's needs and well-being come first. If the family adopts a collective attitude, everyone can learn to be resilient. You lay a solid foundation by starting over: Leave old issues and former disagreements and hurts (including any with sons- and daughters-in-law) where they belong: behind you.

Grandparents should stop telling adult children what to do, and stop questioning their parenting practices. That kind of scrutiny forces an adult child to not only protect herself, but also her growing family. It is the speedy route to undermining any faith she has in leaving her children in a grandparent's care.

When Dot, thirty-eight, a single mother, thought about having her mother live with her to help with her first-grade son, she was worried. "My mother and I had always clashed a lot about most things. She made it clear that she would do things my way, and she did. She was great, and I'll be grateful to her forever."

Although grandparents certainly have more experience in the child-rearing arena, acquiescing to a son or daughter's preferences in regard to their children of any age will smooth the path. Once rules are discussed and established, the hope is that grandparents will abide by them. Parents have every right to raise their children as they see fit.

Arguments about different parenting approaches serve no purpose other than to cause friction or make someone in the family unhappy—parent, grandparent, or child. In the interest of warm camaraderie, it is smart for grandparents to keep quiet. "I try not to say anything. I love what my daughter-in-law does with the children. We disagreed once about toilet training, but I deferred to her. When it comes to raising my grandchildren, she does what she wants and I follow her lead," declares a wise Margery.

Even grandparents who don't like what they're witnessing know it is best to say nothing. Francine isn't always pleased with the way her daughter interacts with her children. "I don't like it when my daughter yells at them or lets them stay up too late. I try to bite my tongue, but I don't always succeed."

When grandparents respect their adult children's authority over the children, they gain their confidence.

When grandparents respect their adult children's authority over the children, they gain their confidence. A grandparent also can increase his or her trust level by avoiding these common grandparent traps.

Grandparent Trap #1: Safety Concerns

Following safety rules is paramount with infants and young children who may not be able to make their needs or problems understood. Safety issues such as diet and designated play areas are not negotiable. Some grandparents think they know more than the parents do; others think their adult children are too safety-conscious. As a grandparent, you may feel your adult child will turn your grandchildren into scared, risk-averse wimps with their seemingly an endless list of worries, safety gadgets, and protective gear.

Lenore Skenazy, author of *Free-Range Kids: Giving Our Children the Freedom We Had Without Going Nuts with Worry,* talks about products with ridiculous claims that overprotective parents buy—baby kneepads, toddler helmets, and bathmats that tell you if the water is too hot. She asks, "A blanket with a built-in headboard? Isn't that what your arm is for? What happened to common sense? Parents are being sold a bill of goods with products like these that feed into parental fears. Grandparents may have to contend with all that silliness."

Child-care practices have changed in the last twenty years, making some parental concerns legitimate. Grandparents should be informed of new approaches to safety, from sleeping positions to feeding protocols and playground rules. Be firm without making a grandparent look or feel as if she is being reckless or irresponsible.

A Parent Might Say:

- "You may think I'm crazy, but I don't feel comfortable (or it makes me nervous) doing it your way."

- "Things have changed since you raised me." (Provide what's changed and how you want a specific safety measure enforced.)

- "Here's an article I read in a magazine (or downloaded from the Internet) that explains the best way to . . ."

- "The doctor feels we should be doing xxx with the baby, or the doctor doesn't want our child doing xxx."

- As a last resort with a stubborn grandparent, you can say, "We want to learn from our own mistakes."

Grandparent Trap #2: Too Much Interference

Too much interference from a grandparent can feel like criticism of adult children's parenting decisions. "Grandma said I could, but Mom and Dad said I couldn't." What's a child to do with such conflicting messages?

Too much interference from a grandparent can feel like criticism of adult children's parenting decisions.

Children learn quickly to play parent against grandparent when the adults don't adhere to the same rules.

Jason, twenty-nine, understood this not months after his grandmother moved in. At the age of ten, he knew, "If I didn't get what I wanted from my mother, I went to my grandmother. If my mother told my grandmother to stop letting me have my way, my grandmother listened for the moment and then gave me whatever I wanted.

"My grandmother is pretty vocal. When my mother tried to tell her something, she would whisper to me, 'I don't want to listen to her; what is she saying?' Her being there made raising me easier for my parents in the day-to-day shopping, cleaning, errands, and that kind of thing, but harder emotionally. My grandmother's philosophy was 'anything goes.' That endeared me to my grandmother, but didn't sit well with my parents."

Grandparents who have settled into their roles often feel as if they can take over reprimanding grandchildren or insist on apologies when a grandchild acts out or is rude. That may be agreed-upon procedure for the times no parent is around; otherwise, allow a parent to handle the problem.

Yolanda recalls: "My son had talked back to his grandfather and my dad was furious. My father wanted me to scold my son and have him apologize in front of the guests we had in the house. I refused. As a child I hated being corrected in front of other people, and I wasn't going to put my son through the same shame and embarrassment. I told my dad that this was my child, and I would talk to him in private."

A Parent Might Say:

- "I appreciate what you do for us and the children, but we would like to address the situation our way." (Then explain how you want something done, or if you would prefer to take care of it yourself.)

- "I know you have the children's best interests at heart, but we can't keep sending different messages. Children need to know the limits."

- "Please don't take my child's side when I am correcting or punishing him. I know you don't mean to do it and want to protect her, but it undermines my job as a parent."

- "If you think I'm being unfair, please tell me later when the children aren't around."

Grandparent Trap #3: Overindulging Grandchildren

For many grandparents, indulging their grandchildren is one of their greatest joys, and parents don't want to take that pleasure away entirely. When grandparents go *Being generous with their time or money is part of grandparenting.* overboard, parents have to underscore the values they want their children to have and ask grandparents to respect their wishes—whether they agree or not. Grandparents will slip; being generous with their time or money is part of grandparenting.

When adult children sanction grandparent indulgence, it's another story. "My husband is dreading the day our three- and four-year-old grandchildren move out. To him it's like having puppy dogs in the house. He pampers them, but my daughter is okay with that. He plays with them for hours. We do have to send my husband to his room before the children's bedtime because he riles them up," says Rita.

If a privilege is occasional, consider letting it go, but if it becomes a regular event and a child begins to expect a parade of excesses, or if leniency obstructs family routines, parents can offer gentle reminders to keep liberties in check.

A Parent Might Say:

- "That is so lovely that you want to do that for the children, but we feel strongly that it's too much."

- "I think he would appreciate that gift more when he's older."

- "It would be better if you gave him part for his birthday and part for the holidays."

- "We understand that grandparents spoil their grandchildren, but can you pull back just a bit?"

- "We are trying hard not to indulge the children. We want them to work for what they get. Will you cooperate with us on this one?"

- "An extra story is terrific now and then or on the weekends, but the children need their sleep. Please get them to bed on time."

- "The children are watching too much television. Here's a list of what we would like them to do instead." (Provide activities that are reasonable for a grandparent to do or supervise.)

Grandparent Trap #4: At Your Beck and Call

So much more goes into living together than just being a comforting presence for grandchildren and a chore-doer for parents. The extra jobs, such as shopping, laundry, and cooking, can become more than a grandparent bargained for. Parents will want to be realistic in what they ask a grandparent, especially a working grandparent, to do. And, grandparents will want to think a request through before committing to be sure it won't add to their anxiety.

Identify obligations before or as soon as you find that you are unhappy or becoming resentful because of all you are doing. It may be that you find yourself babysitting far more than you thought you would, or there's more laundry than you can or want to do. Or, another parent asks if you will include her child in your carpool run. By keeping the lines of communication open with your adult child, you'll be able to explain that you feel you are being taken advantage of. You are the grandparent, not the nanny or a full-time, paid caregiver. That gives you the right to refuse or to renegotiate tasks.

The most important thing you can do is take care of your health and get sufficient rest so that you can help take care of your grandchildren. Ruth tries. "I joined a gym and love going, but I can't get there. I have too much to do with and for my grandchildren."

A Grandparent Might Say:

- "Can we talk about all the driving I'm doing?" Or, "I'm unhappy about . . ."

- "I know you think I can handle xxx, but I'm having trouble."

- "I'd like more help from the children. They're old enough to assist me with xxx. Will you talk to them? Or, we could talk to them together."

- "I'd like some time for myself. Can we figure out how I can get it?"

GRANDPARENTS FILL ESSENTIAL DEVELOPMENTAL ROLES

Just having a grandparent present in the home provides a supportive thread. If parents are caught up in their jobs or distracted by economic worries, grandparents offer continuity. They eliminate disruption of routines and changes in caregivers that can be stressful for young children. In short, live-in grandparents fill in the gaps and provide teaching moments at every turn that help children thrive.

Grandparents offer continuity.

In an e-mail exchange about the economic downturn of 2008–2009, Julie Averill, a former preschool teacher in Manhattan, outlined the changes she saw in two- and three-year-olds in her classroom. "When a young child's daily routine is upset by a parent's job loss or change in caregiver, for example, the child's behavior changes. I noticed overstimulation, regression in separation anxiety and potty-training, and generalized grumpiness."

While parents are at work, grandparents are able to arrange or supervise play dates, another developmental plus for preschoolers. In researching her book, *Child Care Today: Getting*

It Right for Everyone, foremost British child psychologist Penelope Leach found that preschool children who are cared for by grandparents had better language skills.

As children get older, grandparents remain pivotal in their development. For older children, grandparents can be attentive listeners and problem solvers, in addition to providing companionship when parents aren't around. Grandparents can make sure family dinners survive—a ritual many claim is key to teens' avoidance of alcohol, drug, and tobacco use.

On the whole, greater grandparent involvement leads to fewer emotional difficulties and more pro-social behavior among children. In 2009 the *Journal of Family Psychology* reported that benefits for grandchildren were especially significant in single-parent and stepfamily households. According to the study, "Spending time with a grandparent is linked with better social skills and fewer behavior problems among adolescents." Living with grandparents gives children a larger support system and a sense of security—no matter what is happening outside the family, or within it.

WORKING TOGETHER

For the children's sake, make joint decisions to determine what is most worthwhile or useful for a grandchild at any given point. For example, parents and grandparents can discuss appropriate discipline methods, or children's activities. Spend time reviewing everyone's schedule so there are no mix-ups concerning who is looking after the children, and when. Parents should go over how they want grandparents to handle situations to avoid breaking family rules.

Parents may still have to keep after their children to pick up their toys or dream up ways to fend off Grandma's nightly indulgences, but acting as a unit results in often-hard-to-come-by consistency. A group effort also enriches the adult child–parent relationship while it ensures the children are well taken care of and thriving. When you make decisions together, you are much more likely to hear an exuberant child say, "Grandma said I could, *and* so did Mom and Dad!"

PARENTS' CHECKLIST
FOR WORKING TOGETHER

- Don't take advantage of a good thing by overburdening grandparents.
- Pay attention to how your parents are holding up. Watch for signs that you may need to lighten the load.
- Listen attentively to what a grandparent has to say or wants to tell you about your children.
- Admit when you are wrong and a grandparent is correct about something pertaining to your children.
- Acknowledge grandparents' efforts, both large and small.
- Speak favorably about grandparents in front of your children.
- Remind your children that they are to follow their grandparents' instructions.
- Don't be jealous of the time grandparents and grandchildren spend together; it helps you tremendously, and is precious for all concerned.

**GRANDPARENTS' CHECKLIST
FOR WORKING TOGETHER**

- Be willing to give up the control you were used to having when you raised your children.
- Always ask what parents expect, and how they would like each request to be handled.
- Don't try to solve grandchildren's problems by yourself. Ask for advice and input from their parents.
- Include parents in all decisions that affect children's health, happiness, and education.
- When parents are around, don't interfere in issues they have with their children.
- Give a complete and detailed report about a grandchild's day to his parents.
- Offer extra help when you see a parent is preoccupied or exhausted. For instance, review spelling words with a grandchild so a parent can relax after work.
- Don't ever underestimate your contributions; you are needed.

BUILDING BONDS

Grandparents who live with their grandchildren have bonus time to build lasting memories. On the spur of the moment they can tell a story about what Mom or Dad were like or doing at their age, or teach a grandchild how to make cookies or home-made bread from scratch. Grandparents can teach new skills or create something worth boasting about—from learning chess to growing vegetables; from building a birdhouse to making a pizza—whenever there's some free time.

Grandparents are there to pick up on what awakens a child's interest and follow through on it. The luxury to choose the right time is one many grandparents wish they had. Merely being able to have breakfast with a child every morning or share a bit of family history or perpetuate family traditions whenever you feel like it—all serve to fuel the grandparent-grandchild bond.

"As I get older I think family is more important than I did years ago," says George, who is seventy years old. At one time or another, all three of his children have lived at home as adults. He refers to the time one of his sons moved in, along with his wife and two-year-old granddaughter, as "magical. It gave my wife and me the chance to bond with that grandchild. It was delightful.

"We started a tradition when our children were young—tacos every Wednesday night—and have continued it with the grandchildren. Our children and the grandchildren come over for it. It's a leftover benefit from their growing up that will probably continue for generations," George adds.

Family traditions, like teaching moments, are the nucleus of powerful memories and strong links to grandparents. Years ago I wrote *Little Things Mean A Lot: Creating Happy Memories with Your Grandchildren*. The book opens with a credo for grandparents, and applies twofold to grandparents who live with their grandchildren.

The Grandparent Credo

Grandparents give time.

Grandparents give love.

Grandparents give gifts.

Grandparents think big.

Grandparents are good sports.

Grandparents are patient and understanding.

Grandparents are always supportive and enthusiastic.

Grandparents pass on tradition and share their history.

Grandparents don't disagree with parents in front of grandchildren.

Grandparents don't interfere with the upbringing of grandchildren.

Grandparents are devoted to their grandchildren.

Grandparents are fun.

Grandparents are indispensable.

PURE LOVE

Grandparents are indispensable not only to grandchildren, but also to their parents. Relationships with your grandchildren will bring you closer to your adult children. The support is mutually beneficial—to them and to you—and the time together will be recalled warmly by young children, teens, and adults for their entire lives.

Relationships with your grandchildren will bring you closer to your adult children.

The bond starts early, as Ruth implies. "I come down in the morning and I don't know which child to pick up first. We adore them; we laugh all the time. It's pure love."

In a comment to the article, "When Grandma Can't Be Bothered," posted on *The New York Times* Web site, one grandfather wrote, "Our two-and-a-half-year-old granddaughter and her parents live with us. Her dad is a stay-at-home parent (and a good one at that). I love it. We help with babysitting when the need arises . . . I see her in the morning when she's waking up and just wants to cuddle for a while. I play hide-and-seek, peekaboo, read kiddie books, and make up silly, funny, phantasmagoric stories. With apologies to Lou Gehrig, I am the luckiest of men."

At whatever age they begin, grandparent-grandchild bonds endure. Jacqui's rocky relationship with her mother-in-law had little effect on her son's connection to his grandmother, which began when he was in elementary school. Her son is almost thirty now, and her mother-in-law is almost ninety. "To this day, they are very protective of each other," says Jacqui. "It's a loving relationship that formed from the simple things she did for him. She didn't drive just my son where he wanted to go; most of the kids in the neighborhood tagged along. He and his friends remember the adventures she took them on, too, and visit her. She has a special place in all their hearts and memory banks, but especially in my son's."

Chapter Thirteen

You Can Go Home Again

LIFE SELDOM GOES AS EFFORTLESSLY OR PERFECTLY AS IMAGINED. We set a path or think about the one we'll follow, and rarely is it exactly as we pictured. As we travel a desired route, we get diverted by unanticipated twists and turns. With each setback comes an opportunity, none greater than the chance to become closer to family. Even if you hadn't thought about relying on your parents or asking your adult child or sibling for help, it's comforting to know that you have a fallback position, a place to regroup when life skids off course.

Figuring out where you want to be next and how to get there is a process. While you search, in a world that couldn't care less, it's comforting to have people who do care and on whom you can depend. Those who have gone home again or moved into their children's homes are glad they did, even if initially they were hesitant, unsure it would be a good experience. And, those who took them in are happy that they didn't bar the doors or send money so their relatives could stay where they were. They maneuvered around their relationship kinks and managed glaring differences they once thought irreconcilable. In the end, you are willing when someone in the family needs you. In the process you reinforce affection and create family solidarity in the calm of not worrying about a teen out too late or a parent who might need emergency assistance.

What Your Parent May Be Thinking

"I didn't know when my children moved back in with me how much I would enjoy them. I saw their return as an opportunity to have a closer relationship and to get to know them better. It's a chance parents don't usually get."

Elaine's son moved home at twenty-seven, her daughter at thirty.

The New Normal

For the last four decades, living together again as adults was something many had difficulty accepting. Fortunately, today, it is not only accepted, but it's also become a growing norm in our society. Just a few years ago parents still focused on how to stop enabling adult children and were unsure of how much or how little they should offer in the way of assistance. One of the driving principles was to not let adult children return home. A similar attitude prevailed around having parents move in with

---

What What Your Adult Child May Be Thinking

"My parents are giving up a lot to have me stay here. I respect that. At times I'm torn between wanting to be with my friends and wanting to be with my parents. I know time with them is precious. When I get married and have kids, I may only see them twice a year for holidays."

Kate, twenty-six, moved home after living by herself for several years.

---

their adult children. What parents and their grown-up children would miss by holding on to those beliefs!

In recent years, we've taken a page from other cultures, in which multiple generations have always been inclined to live together. Carlos, forty, recently returned home to live with his mother in order to save money while starting up a new business. He talks about his Latin heritage: "We have a pattern of family being tight. Adult children play out their familial roles."

Carlos categorizes the arrangement of single adult children living at home as the "default" position, not the exception. In Latin families, he says, "The question is not why you are living with your parents, but rather, why aren't you?"

In many Asian cultures, respecting elders, family staying connected, and fulfilling family obligations remain central values. That means being there for family whether or not there's a critical reason. African American families also continue their pattern of multigenerational living, seeing family support as a virtue. This is an attitude more and more people of all cultures are adopting.

Ann, who was married for thirty years and has shared her childhood home with her mother for the past three years, accurately notes, "Mom and I became a statistic adding up to a new trend in the census and other studies. Adults are increasingly moving back with—or never leaving—their parents. I told my mother that living with her might actually be superior to living with a husband."

When it comes to feelings about sharing living quarters, it doesn't seem to make a difference if the stay is open-ended, date-specific, or permanent—or if it is voluntary or involuntary.

Kimberly, forty-three, bought her childhood home and is fast to let you know that "it comes with my father, who is my favorite person in the world. That's an unusual bonus." She is waiting for an adoption to finalize, and then the baby will join them.

During the 1950s and 1960s, medical researchers discovered that residents of Roseto, Pennsylvania, had a significantly lower mortality rate from heart disease than the rest of the country—a phenomenon called "The Roseto Effect." At the time of the study, Roseto was a community of Italian immigrants, *all* of whom lived in multigenerational families. The original study and later studies of "The Roseto Effect" concluded that cooperation and support among Roseto family members and within the larger community reduced stress and the heart problems it creates.

In addition to health benefits, most agree that having the chance to build closer family ties is a gift. The desire to form friendships between parents and sons and daughters, and to strengthen bonds with grandchildren make it easy to understand why being under one roof again is "the new normal," and will continue to be, no matter what the American economy does.

Having the chance to build closer family ties is a gift.

Given that people live longer, and in good health, you will have many years to appreciate the reward for your effort.

ALL GROWN UP AND A PLACE TO GO

The pressure cooker environment in which most of us live can be filled with disappointments that leave many in limbo.

Family helps surmount barriers and makes a daunting road easier to navigate. Undoubtedly you will have concerns from time to time. An adult child coming home may feel as if his life is moving in reverse. A parent welcoming his adult child with open arms may feel he has to give up newfound freedom just when he was geared up to retire and travel. With extra people to support, he may have to live more frugally. Accommodation is called for on everyone's part.

Coexisting happily requires shying away from the small things that destroy relationships. Avoid focusing on petty behaviors or perceived shortcomings you once found grating. The obsessive parent or adult child, for example, overlooks sloppiness or a forgotten errand. Parents and adult children who are motivated to build their relationship accept that they don't always have to be right about every detail or incident— that relating well and getting along are far more important. Rita uses a no-conflict approach with good reason: "Exploding is not worth it. I don't want to lose my daughter, son-in-law, or grandchildren."

When families address the "big picture," the relationship can move forward in a positive direction. Parents become more accommodating when they no longer have to parent; adult children take on more responsibility when they stop acting like children. Jeremy, thirty-three, agrees: "My parents were more open once they saw me as an adult. I was able to talk to them as adults once I realized it was a mutual relationship now."

NEW VIEWS FOR
ADULT CHILDREN TO ADOPT

- Be a realist and think: I pay a small amount (or no rent) and get to save the rest.
- I have good meals and a sympathetic ear to listen to my troubles.
- My family is a source of good advice; most likely their guidance will be beneficial.
- This is a better deal than I could possibly "cut" on my own right now.
- For the most part, the "push and pull" of being parented has ended.
- I need to give my parents room to act like parents every now and then.
- I can interact with my parents and get to know— and enjoy—them as people, not just as parents.

NEW VIEWS FOR PARENTS TO ADOPT

- I have company and an extra set of helping hands.
- I can fill in the day-to-day gaps for my son or daughter and his or her family.
- My adult child is safe and sheltered, and I don't have to worry that he's broke and wandering.
- I can compensate for the years I wasn't available or wasn't the parent I had planned to be.
- My parenting days are over. Now is the time to enjoy my grown-up children.

Expect Less, Get More

Living together again is a new opportunity to be a family in every sense of the word. Relationships evolve into much more than they were, despite the occasional problems. As much as we would like to think otherwise, disappointments and arguments are inevitable in every family.

The grass always seems greener at someone else's house. The grandmother who sees her grandchildren every few months wants to be geographically and emotionally closer, while the grandmother who lives with her grandchildren can give you a laundry list of complaints. The twenty-something living on her own and struggling to pay her rent wishes she had what her best friend enjoys: parents who put a roof over her head, and all the meals she can eat on the table—and it doesn't cost her friend a dime.

Don't feel guilty if you have days when you think you would like to be alone or don't want all the new diversions or disruptions that are unavoidable when "new" people join a household. You may have days when you find the interference of a parent, daughter or daughter-in-law, or grandchildren more intrusive than others. Consider that you may be too involved. Remember, life runs best when it runs parallel to, not interlocked with, the people you love.

Sharing space again as adults changes views and delivers insights into the people you thought knew so well. It also stirs emotions. Joyce, sixty-four, whose twenty-six-year-old son lives at home, says, "When I'm not worried about Jeffrey's lack of work, we enjoy having dinner together. It's nice to be close to him again. It makes me want my older child, whom I only see once a year, to come home, too. I miss him."

Twenty-nine-year-old Nina and her husband lived with her parents for two years and learned a lot about her parents. "I ended up with an inside view of my parents' relationship and have more respect for what my mom does for my dad. The tables have turned. My mother asks me for advice. Ours became much more a friendship than them parenting me."

Being a friend with a parent can trickle down into relationships with other family members. Carlos confesses to being "underdeveloped in the caring area. Living with my mother made me look beyond myself, and that enhanced my relationship with my sister, who is around for Mom when I can't be. My sister and I are beyond family now—we're good friends."

> *Being a friend with a parent can trickle down into relationships with other family members.*

FOR THE LONG OR SHORT HAUL

The willingness to bend when necessary, to pitch in when needed (and to back off when not) turns family relationships into enduring friendships. Whether you're a twenty-five-year-old or sixty-year-old adult child going home, or a parent or in-law moving in, you can minimize the friction and maximize the camaraderie by following the Cardinal Rules for Living Together. These basic guidelines work whether you are home for a month, a year, ten years, or permanently. They bring the results you want: harmony, happiness, love, and encouragement from the parent, adult child, or sibling you are relearning to live with.

The long haul doesn't necessarily mean you will live together forever. By sticking to the Cardinal Rules, you preserve the relationship that develops for as long as you stay, or wherever you live in the future. The bond is an intangible you take and always keep with you.

THE CARDINAL RULES FOR LIVING TOGETHER

- Be realistic about what you expect and how each family member can help.
- Don't let money problems cloud personal feelings.
- Be grateful and make concessions.
- Keep your boundaries strong and respect those of others.
- Don't rehash past negatives. Move on.
- Use humor to ease sticky situations.
- Be understanding of the difficult problems a relative faces.
- Retain a "We're in this together" attitude while holding on to your separate life.
- Focus on all the good things you share.

SURPRISING OUTCOMES: I'M STILL HERE

Few things in life are black and white, and living together as grown-ups is no exception. As Linda, sixty, speaking about her return to her parents' home a few years ago, reminds us, "I had to give up some of my independence. I have to negotiate who gets to watch what shows on TV, and I'm urged to call if I'm going to be late, but I adjusted."

Once you get past the minor hurdles and accept the major differences, the future as a renewed nuclear family is full of revelations. I asked the people I spoke with what surprised them the most about living with their mothers, fathers, sons, or daughters again. What they said is a testament to reinventing your relationship and turning it into a richer one.

You may have strong opinions that do not necessarily gel with those of your parent or adult child, because adult children are not necessarily clones of their parents. Linda, the self-proclaimed rebel in her family, strongly urges adult children to live with their parents. "Do it even if you are very different from your parents," she insists.

Despite using the word "horrible" to describe communication between herself and her mother and stepfather—communication that sometimes included screaming matches—Sophia finds the bright side, and puts the worst aspects of living with them to rest. "I had a shoulder to cry on when I was in the dumps about my failed marriage," says Sophia. "My mother was an absentee mom when I was growing up. She didn't even know my favorite color. Now she knows my favorite color, what kind of books I like, and my exercise regime. We've had a lot of good laughs and companionship time. We've gotten closer, although I'll never be her and she'll never be me."

Parents who respect that their children are adults have an easier time relearning to live with them. Parents or adult children may be angry at the point they start living together. Once they move past the irritation, they begin enjoying each other. Conversations turn pleasant and satisfaction reigns.

Unemployed for months and living at home, Melissa, twenty-six, has parents who recognize her adulthood. "It's wonderful to sit with them at breakfast and chat. It's surprising how easy it is for me to be an adult with my parents."

Margery's son, wife, and grandchildren moved to their own home a few years ago. How she still feels underscores what people say who have experienced living with immediate family again. "I miss them terribly. I would do it again in a heartbeat."

Parents and adult children alike are sad when someone in the family moves out and goes off in a new direction. Adult children fully grasp that they will probably never live with their parents again. And, after enjoying each other and building a friendship, many parents get teary-eyed or cry at the mere mention of a departure. Moving in together is a huge step, and moving on to live independently is a bigger and more challenging one.

Talking about leaving and doing it are unrelated; those who can, stall and find reasons to stay. The response I heard most often from those who lived with family for a year or two, as well as those with arrangements lasting decades, was, "I'm still here." Even people who think that joining forces is temporary often end up staying, because the arrangement works to everyone's advantage, and because they love each other in spite of occasional strife or unpleasantness. They make it work, and preserve their good feelings for each other.

The most lasting relationships are between parents and children or between siblings. There is no place like home for building and savoring these irreplaceable, lifelong connections. No one has any of those to spare.

Resources and Related Reading

Introduction

Generational Differences. Survey Brief: Pew Hispanic Center and Kaiser Family Foundation, March 2004, http://pewhispanic.org/files/fact sheets/13.pdf.

Merz, Eva-Maria, Frans J. Oort, Ezgi Ozeke-Kocabas, and Carlo Schuengel. "Intergenerational Family Solidarity: Value Differences between Immigrant Groups and Generations," *Journal of Family Psychology* 23(3), June 2009, pp. 291–300.

Sutherland, Tucker. "Once Again There Will Be a Grandparents Day that Few Will Notice," Grandparent News: SeniorJournal.com, August 27, 2007, www.seniorjournal.com/NEWS/Grandparents/2007/7-08-27-OnceAgain.htm.

Tuna, Cari. "For '09 Grads, Job Prospects Take a Dive," *The Wall Street Journal,* October 22, 2008, http://online.wsj.com/article/SB122464 035263357361.html.

Chapter 1: The Art of Living Together

Gibbs, Nancy. "Thrift Nation," *Time,* April 27, 2009, pp. 20–31.

Lee, William Poy. E-mail correspondence, September 22, 2009.

Shetterly, Caitlin. "Recession Diary: The Long and Winding Road Home." National Public Radio Weekend Edition, May 16, 2009, www .npr.org/ templates/story/story.php?storyId=104131481&ps=rs.

Winerip, Michael. "The Family that Job-Hunts Together," *The New York Times,* May 8, 2009, www.nytimes.com/2009/05/10/fashion/10 generationb.html.

Related Reading:

Faber, Adele and Elaine Mazlish. *Siblings Without Rivalry: How to Help Your Children Live Together So You Can Live Too (Expanded Edition).* New York: Harper Paperbacks, 2004.

Fleck, Carole. "All Under One Roof," *AARP Bulletin,* May 2009, pp. 22–25.

Lee, William Poy. *The Eighth Promise: An American Son Pays Tribute to His Toisanese Mother.* Emmaus, PA: Rodale, 2007 (www.TheEighth Promise.com).

Wadler, Joyce. "Caught in the Safety Net," *The New York Times,* May 13, 2009, www.nytimes.com/2009/05/14/garden/14return.html.

CHAPTER 3: GREAT (AND NOT SO GREAT) EXPECTATIONS

Brown, Heidi. "Hi Mom! I'm . . . Back!" Forbes.com, May 14, 2009, www.forbes.com/2009/05/14/adult-kids-moving-home-forbes-woman-time-family.html.

CHAPTER 4: MONEY MATTERS

Kobliner, Beth. "When the Kids Move Back In: Offer a Financial Safety Net that's Comfortable, But Not Too Comfortable," *Money,* June 9, 2009, http://money.cnn.com/2009/06/08/pf/move_back_home.moneymag/index.htm.

"People: The Younger Generation," *Time,* November 5, 1951, www.time.com/time/magazine/article/0,9171,856950,00.html.

Silverstein, Merril and Conroy, Stephen. "Does Having a Good Relationship with Your Children Pay Off?" The Longitudinal Study of Generations. University of Southern California, 2000, www.usc.edu/dept/gero/research/ 4gen/conroy.htm.

Trejos, Nancy. "Toll on 401(k) Savings Adds Years More of Toil," *The Washington Post,* January 29, 2009, www.washingtonpost.com/wpdyn/content/article/2009/01/28/AR2009012800900.html.

RELATED READING:

Haughney, Christine. "Parental Lifelines, Frayed to Breaking," *The New York Times,* June 7, 2009, www.nytimes.com/2009/06/08/nyregion/08trustafarians. html.

Kobliner, Beth. *Get a Financial Life: Personal Finance in Your Twenties and Thirties.* New York: Fireside, 2009.

———. "Support Your Struggling Grads: Kids Having Trouble Paying Back Student Loans? Help Out without Shelling Out," *Money,* June 24, 2009, http://money.cnn.com/2009/06/18/pf/college/student_loans.moneymag/index.htm.

Lieber, Ron. "When Fledglings Return to the Nest," *The New York Times,* July 11, 2009, pp. B1, B5.

Luo, Michael. "Still Working, But Forced to Make Do With Less," *The New York Times,* May 29, 2009, pp. A1, A17.

Marksjarvis, Gail. "Target Date Funds Took Too Many Risks for Near-Retirees," *The Chicago Tribune,* March 22, 2009, http://archives.chicagotribune.com/2009/mar/22/business/ chi-ym-target-0322-cpmar22.

"The Silent Generation Revisited," *Time,* June 29, 1970, www.time .com/time/magazine/article/0,9171,878847,00.html.

CHAPTER 5: PUSHING YOUR BUTTONS

Canellos, Peter, ed. *Last Lion: The Fall and Rise of Ted Kennedy.* New York: Simon & Schuster, 2009, p. 104.

CHAPTER 6: FROM BEDROOM TO DEN AND BACK AGAIN

Wadler, Joyce. "Caught in the Safety Net," *The New York Times,* May 14, 2009, www.nytimes.com/2009/05/14/garden/14return .html?_r=2&pagewanted1.

CHAPTER 7: TOGETHER AND APART

RELATED READING:

"Create the Good" (volunteer opportunities by where you live and what you would like to do). American Association of Retired Persons, www.createthegood.org (updates can be sent directly to your e-mail address).

"Volunteer Match" (volunteer opportunities by zip code and keywords), www.volunteermatch.org.

CHAPTER 9: HOMEWARD BOUND AT TWENTY-SOMETHING

Brown, Heidi. "Hi Mom! I'm . . . Back!" Forbes.com, May 14, 2009, www .forbes.com/2009/05/14/adult-kids-moving-home-forbes-woman-time-family.html.

"College Hiring Falls 22 Percent." Spotlight Online: National Association of Colleges and Employers, March 4, 2009, www.naceweb.org/ spotlight/2009/e030409.htm.

Cooper, Lauren. "Yale Study: Starting Career during Recession Can Damage Salary for Decades," DailyFinance.com, September 25, 2009, www.dailyfinance.com/2009/09/25/ yale-study-starting-career-during-recession-can-damage-salary-f/.

"In-Depth Research Reveals How Sex, Money, Race, Faith, Family and Technology Affect the Current and Future Happiness of America's Youth." MTV and the Associated Press, August 20, 2007, www.mtv .com/thinkmtv/research.

Jayson, Sharon. "Parents, Kids Today More in Harmony than Prior Generations," *USA Today,* August 12, 2009, www.usatoday.com/news/ nation/2009-08-12-generation-gap-pew_N.htm.

Kohut, Andrew. "A Portrait of 'Generation Next': How Young People View Their Lives, Futures and Politics." The Pew Research Center, January 9, 2007, http://people-press.org/reports/pdf/300.pdf.

Marano, Hara Estroff (editor at large). *Psychology Today* magazine. Telephone interview, May 5, 2009.

Newman, Susan. *The Book of NO: 250 Ways to Say It—and Mean It and Stop People-Pleasing Forever.* New York: McGraw-Hill, 2006.

Pugh, Tony. "Recession's Toll: Most Recent College Grads Working Low-Skill Jobs," McClatchy Newspapers, Washington Bureau, June 25, 2009, www.mcclatchydc.com/homepage/v-print/story/70788.html.

Tapscott, Don. *Grown Up Digital: How the Net Generation Is Changing Your World.* New York: McGraw-Hill, 2009.

Taylor, Paul, and Richard Morin. "Forty Years After Woodstock: A Gentler Generation Gap," A Social & Demographic Trend Report, August 12, 2009, http://pewsocialtrends.org/assets/pdf/after-woodstock-gentler-generation-gap.pdf.

"2009 College Graduates Moving Back Home in Larger Numbers," CollegeGrad.com, www.collegegrad.com/press/2009_college_ graduates_moving_back_home_in_larger_numbers.shtml.

Warnack, Heather Harlan. "College Grads Are Moving Back Home with Mom and Dad: Recent Grads Struggle to Land Jobs in Recession," *Baltimore Business Journal,* May 22, 2009, http://baltimore .bizjournals.com/baltimore/stories/ 2009/05/25/smallb1.html.

RELATED READING:

Echols, Tucker. "Job Market Shrinking for College Grads," *Baltimore Business Journal,* May 12, 2009, http://baltimore.bizjournals.com/ baltimore/stories/ 2009/05/11/daily15.html.

Furman, Elina. *Boomerang Nation: How to Survive Living with Your Parents . . . the Second Time Around.* New York: Fireside, 2005.

Gordon, Linda Pearlman, and Susan Morris Shaffer. *Mom, Can I Move Back In With You?: A Survival Guide for Parents of Twenty-Somethings.* New York: Tarcher, 2004.

Marano, Hara Estroff. *A Nation of Wimps: The High Cost of Invasive Parenting.* New York: Broadway Books, 2008.

VanderMey, Anne. "College Grads Facing Worst Hiring Climate Since 2002," *Business Week,* March 2009, www.businessweek.com/managing/blogs/ first_jobs/archives/2009/03/college_grads_f.html.

Williams, Alex. "Say Hello to Underachieving: A Generation Used to Summer Internships and Trips to Italy Faces Long, Hot Days Learning to Kick Back," *The New York Times,* July 5, 2009, pp. ST1, ST7.

Willis, Gerri. "College Graduates Move Back Home," CNNMoney.com, July 23, 2009, http://money.cnn.com/2009/07/23/pf/saving/graduates_move_back_home/ index.htm.

Job Search Web Sites:

CollegeRecruiter.com, www.collegerecruiter.com (internships for college students and entry-level jobs for recent graduates).

Vault.com, www.vault.com/wps/portal/usa (basic free membership provides industry newsletters, ability to apply for jobs, and discussion groups).

Chapter 10: Older and Headed Home

Gardner, Marilyn. "Adult Children Back in the Nest: The Economic Downturn Is One Reason Families Are Combining Households," *The Christian Science Monitor,* February 4, 2009, www.csmonitor.com/2009/0224/p17s01-lifp.html.

Witchel, Alex. "The Novels of Colm Toibin—Including His Latest, Set in Brooklyn—Are All about Searching for Home: His Irish Diaspora," *The New York Times,* May 3, 2009, www.nytimes.com/2009/05/03/magazine/03toibin-t.html.

Related Reading:

Shetterly, Caitlin. "A Man, Woman, Baby and an Empty Bank Account." National Public Radio, March 21, 2009, www.npr.org/templates/story/story.php?storyId=102062255.

Chapter 11: Parents and In-Laws Moving In

Ebeling, Ashlea. "How to Set Up a Multi-Generation Household," *Forbes magazine,* May 25, 2009, www.forbes.com/forbes/2009/0525/066-investment-guide-09-save-big-move-grandma-in.html.

Green, Penelope. "Your Mother Is Moving In? That's Great," *The New York Times,* January 14, 2009, www.nytimes.com/2009/01/15/garden/15mothers.html.

Kotlikoff, Laurence J. "Should You Move In With Your Mom? Multigenerational living produces dramatic savings, economist says," *Forbes magazine,* May 10, 2009, www.forbes.com/2009/05/10/savings-living-with-mom-personal-finance-retirement-kotlikoff.html.

Newman, Susan. *Nobody's Baby Now: Reinventing Your Adult Relationship with Your Mother and Father.* New York: Walker & Company, 2003.

Related Reading:

Forward, Susan. *Toxic In-Laws: Loving Strategies for Protecting Your Marriage.* San Francisco: Harper, 2002.

Horgan, David, and Shira Block. *When Your Parent Moves In: Every Adult Child's Guide to Living with an Aging Parent.* Avon, MA: Adams Media, 2009.

Ilardo, Joseph A., and Carole R. Rothman. *Are Your Parents Driving You Crazy? Getting to Yes with Competent, Aging Parents* (2nd Ed.). Acton, MA: VanderWyk & Burnham, 2005.

Chapter 12: "Grandma Said I Could"

Attar-Schwartz, Shalhevet, Jo-Pei Tan, Ann Buchanan, Eirini Flouri, and Julia Griggs. "Grandparenting and Adolescent Adjustment in Two-Parent Biological, Lone-Parent, and Step-Families," *Journal of Family Psychology* 23(1), 2009, 67–75.

Averill, Julie. Kidsatworknyc.com and former preschool teacher. E-mail correspondence, August 28, 2009.

The Eleanor Roosevelt Papers. "Sara Delano Roosevelt (1854–1941)." Eleanor Roosevelt National Historic Site. Hyde Park, New York, 2003, www.nps.gov/archive/elro/glossary/roosevelt-sara-delano.htm.

Kaufman, Joanne. "When Grandma Can't Be Bothered," *The New York Times,* March 4, 2009, www.nytimes.com/2009/03/05/fashion/05grandparents-1.html? _r=2.

Leach, Penelope. *Child Care Today: Getting It Right for Everyone.* New York: Knopf, 2009.

National Center on Addiction and Substance Abuse (CASA). "The Importance of Family Dinners V." Columbia University, New York. September, 2009, www.casacolumbia.org/absolutenm/articlefiles/380-Importance%20of%20 Family%20Dinners%20V.pdf.

Newman, Susan. *Little Things Mean a Lot: Creating Happy Memories with Your Grandchildren.* New York: Crown, 1996.

Skenazy, Lenore. Author of *Free-Range Kids.* E-mail correspondence, August 25, 2009.

Swarns, Rachel L. " 'Family Friendly' White House Proves Less So for Many Aides," *The New York Times,* July 4, 2009, pp. A1, A13.

RELATED READING:

Ruiz, S. A. and M. Silverstein. "Relationships with Grandparents and the Emotional Well-Being of Late Adolescence and Young Adult Children," *Journal of Social Issues* 63, 2007, pp. 793–808.

Shipman, Claire, Susan Rucci, and Imaeyen Ibanga. "The First Grandma: Who Is Marian Robinson? Michelle Obama's Mother Has Uprooted Her Life to Help Raise Her Grandchildren." ABC News, January 22, 2008. http://abcnews.go.com /GMA/Inauguration/story?id=6703161&page=1.

Skenazy, Lenore. *Free-Range Kids: Giving Our Children the Freedom We Had Without Going Nuts With Worry.* San Francisco: Jossey-Bass, 2009.

Zullo, Kathryn and Allan Zullo. *A Boomer's Guide to Grandparenting.* Kansas City: Andrews McMeel, 2004.

CHAPTER 13: YOU CAN GO HOME AGAIN

Egolf, Brenda, Judith Lasker, Stewart Wolf, and Louise Potvin. "The Roseto Effect: A 50-Year Comparison of Mortality Rates," *American Journal of Public Health* 82(8), August 1992, pp. 1089–1092, www .ncbi.nlm.nih.gov/pmc/articles/ PMC1695733/pdf/amjph00545-0027. pdf.

Juang, Linda P., and Jeffrey T. Cookston. "A Longitudinal Study of Family Obligation and Depressive Symptoms among Chinese American Adolescents," *Journal of Family Psychology* 23(3), June 2009, pp. 396–404.

RELATED READING:

"Coping with Life's Stressors." The Cleveland Clinic, http://my.cleveland
  clinic.org/healthy_living/stress_management/hic_coping_with_lifes_
  stressors.aspx.

Ehrenreich, Barbara. "A Homespun Safety Net," *The New York Times,* July
  12, 2009, p. 9.

Hutter, Mark. *The Changing Family* (3rd Ed.). Boston: Allyn & Bacon,
  1998.

Kotkin, Joel. "There's No Place Like Home," *Newsweek,* October 19,
  2009, pp. 42–43.

Acknowledgments

Very much like a family living together again happily as adults, writing a nonfiction book is a collaborative effort. Highest on the list of people to recognize for their contributions are the men and women who talked with me about their lives and situations, their family relationships, and their experiences living together. Because they spoke with me anonymously, I can't thank them by name. You know who you are. I am grateful for your time, stories, and observations . . . and grateful to Carla Van Dyck who efficiently kept track of everyone.

In the publishing world, the starting point for most books from evaluating the writer's initial idea to its arrival in the bookstore is the literary agent. Without my agent, Carol Mann, *Under One Roof Again* might still be a pile of pages on my desk. For seeing its possibilities and expertly shepherding it through the process of becoming a book, thank you Mary Norris, editorial director at Globe Pequot Press. Mary's skills smoothed the process, and her insights greatly improved the book.

Someone has to pull all the editorial and production pieces together. Thank you to Ellen Urban, who was the book's project editor; to Melissa Hayes, who copyedited it; and to those who work behind the scenes at Globe Pequot Press. In the final analysis, they are as essential as the people with whom I spoke and whose personal details and private thoughts you just read. A final note of gratitude: *Under One Roof Again* is first and foremost a tribute to my family for their understanding and positive ways of relating. I would happily live with any one of you again.

INDEX

finances
  adult children contributions,
    58–61
  barter system contributions, 64–65
  college graduates, 140–41, 148–49
  expectations *vs.* conflicts, 51–54,
    60–61, 63–64, 66–67
  generational attitudes toward,
    55–58
  inheritance issues, 14
  parent contributions, 61–62,
    62–63
  pooling resources, 62–63
  as reason for co-habitation, 2, 3,
    50–53
  showing appreciation, 64
  taking advantage and resentment,
    13–14, 51, 54, 61
  tips for, 67
First Grandmas, 187–89
flexibility, 16, 18
food preferences, 27–28, 181
Forbes magazine, 140
Free-Range Kids (Skenazy), 192
friends
  core elements of friendship, 168
  criticism of, 81, 86
  parents and children as, 167–70
  for socializing opportunities, 112,
    113–14, 118, 119–21

generational differences, 15, 55–58
Generation Next, 144
girlfriends, live-in, 135–36
grandchildren. *See* children
    (grandchildren)
grandparents
  benefits of, 186–87, 201–4
  as caregivers for grandchildren,
    187–90

child development and, 198–99
  disadvantages of, 188
  grandchildren's responsibility
    for, 184
  parenting practices and trust
    building, 190–98
  as role models, 185
  working together tips, 200–201
Grown Up Digital (Tapscott), 138
guilt, 16, 21, 82–85

helicopter parents, 143–44
hoarding, 100

illness, 166–67
independence
  activities and entertainment, 116,
    120–21
  assessments of, 19
  benefits of, 121
  breaks from family, 109–13,
    115, 117
  of parents and in-laws, 178–79
  schedule monitoring and, 116
  socializing, 113–14, 118, 119–20
  tips encouraging, 119
inheritance concerns, 14
in-laws. *See also* grandparents;
    parents
  benefits, 171–74
  household contributions, 178–79
  living together tips, 177, 184
  pre-moving in communication,
    174–75
  quirks and difficulties, 180–84
  as role models for grandchildren,
    184–85
  trial periods, 174
  understanding, 176–77

ABOUT THE AUTHOR

Social psychologist and best-selling author Dr. Susan Newman specializes in issues that affect children, family life, and relationships. She taught at Rutgers University in New Jersey, and has written many popular books, among them, *The Book of NO: 250 Ways to Say It—and Mean It and Stop People-Pleasing Forever, Parenting An Only Child: The Joys and Challenges of Raising Your One and Only, Little Things Long Remembered: Making Your Children Feel Special Every Day,* and *Nobody's Baby Now: Reinventing Your Adult Relationship with Your Mother and Father.* Several of her books have become award-winning educational videos.

Dr. Newman is a frequent speaker on parenting, work-life balance, and human behavior. She writes for *Psychology Today* magazine on family life, focusing on parenting and the issues around raising and being an only child. You can read her work at: http://blogs.psychologytoday.com/blog/singletons.

Her research and knowledge of family relationships and parenting have led to features in *Time* magazine, *Redbook, Harvard* magazine, *Self, Woman's Day, Cosmopolitan, Parents,* and many other leading magazines and newspapers, including *The New York Times* and *USA Today.* She appears often on television and radio—both nationally and locally—including The Today Show, Good Morning America, 20/20, *NBC Nightly News,* ABC World News Tonight, CNN News, FOX News, NPR's *Talk of the Nation,* and talk shows in major cities discussing breaking news and family problems.

Dr. Newman is a member of the American Psychological Association, the Authors Guild, and the American Association of Journalists and Authors. She lives in New Jersey, where she is a Court-Appointed Special Advocate (CASA) for abused and neglected children. She has one son from her second marriage and four stepchildren from her first—all of whom are welcome to return home at any time—and five stepgrandchildren.

For information related to *Under One Roof Again* and Susan Newman's other books, television and radio appearances, and articles, visit her Web site at www.susannewmanphd.com.